DEAN
ARKA

WITHDRAWN
From the
Dean B. Ellis Library
Arkansas State University

THE CLASH OF
PROGRESS AND SECURITY

Also published in

REPRINTS OF ECONOMIC CLASSICS

BY ALLAN G. B. FISHER
SOME PROBLEMS OF WAGES AND THEIR REGULATION IN GREAT
BRITAIN SINCE 1918 [1926]

THE CLASH OF
PROGRESS AND SECURITY

BY

ALLAN G. B. FISHER

PROFESSOR OF ECONOMICS
IN THE UNIVERSITY OF OTAGO

REPRINTS OF ECONOMIC CLASSICS

Augustus M. Kelley · Publishers
NEW YORK · 1966

First Published 1935

Library of Congress Catalogue Card Number

66-21369

Printed in the United States of America
by Sentry Press, New York, N. Y. 10019

HB
171
.F53
1966

PREFACE

THE germ of the ideas which are defended in this book first developed in the author's mind in the atmosphere of intellectual discomfort created by the attempt to reconcile with the teachings of elementary economic science the view, at one time so common in Australia and New Zealand as to be practically universal, that any policy of sound economic development in "new" countries must provide for an indefinite expansion of rural population engaged in agricultural and pastoral work. This widely held view appeared to be so much at variance with what might reasonably be expected in a world where the rate of population growth was slowing down at the same time as the efficiency of production of foodstuffs and raw materials was rapidly increasing, that a brief attack on the whole position, under the title "The Bogey of the Urban Drift", was written in September 1926 for the *New Zealand Highway*, now unhappily defunct but at that time the journal of the Workers' Educational Association in New Zealand: "Instead of deploring the urban drift, we ought to rejoice at the evidence which it affords that the primary necessities of the whole population can be supplied by a steadily diminishing proportion of the people". The same thesis was developed in greater detail in an article on "The Drift to the Towns", published in November 1929 in the *Economic Record*, the journal of the Economic Society of Australia and New Zealand : " An increase in the number of farmers is not a suitable method for improving the economic

v

148657

position of those who are already farmers. . . . As a community grew in wealth the proportion of farming to total population would steadily diminish. . . . To complain about the world-wide drift to the towns is to complain that the world as a whole is growing richer."

During the year 1931 I had an opportunity to make a study of the changes in relative incomes paid for different kinds of work in recent years, and it became clear that the problem which had originally presented itself as one of the relative rates of growth of rural and urban population was in fact much wider in its scope and significance. Improvements in the capacity for wealth-production, and in particular in education standards, were likely not only to stimulate a relatively rapid growth of urban population, but also a diminution of the customary differentials between the wages paid for skilled and unskilled labour. This point was elaborated in the *International Labour Review* in June 1932, in an article on "Education and Relative Wage Rates".

During recent years most economists, whatever their reading habits may have been in the past, have felt it necessary to pay increasing attention to the work of Böhm-Bawerk. His refusal to include in his theory of capital any consideration of what would happen if in the future men turned to types of consumption different from those which had been customary in the past (a change which was obviously certain to occur if standards of production were improved), strengthened the impression which had been growing in my mind, that it was impossible to reach sound judgments on matters of practical policy unless we thought constantly in terms of the changes in the structure of production, in the distribution of labour and capital which were demanded by improvements in the general efficiency of production. Reflection upon this theme led to my writing an article on "Capital and the Growth of Knowledge" which appeared in the *Economic Journal* in September 1933; and the present work is an attempt to expound in a more systematic way the general problems which inevitably develop in any formulation of a concrete picture of the implications of material progress for the structure and organisation of industry as a whole.

Any reader who is familiar with the work of the late Professor Cannan will readily appreciate the extent of my debt to his teaching. It was he who first convinced me that the study of economic theory was something more than a mere intellectual toy, combining as he did a sturdy realistic common-sense with a profound understanding of the foundations of thought in economic science. It has not infrequently happened that, when I had imagined that I had in my own thinking come upon some neat or novel point, I have discovered that the same point had already been made by the late Professor Cannan in a sentence or paragraph which I had already read, but whose source I had forgotten.

Many points in this book have been discussed from time to time with friends in Australia and New Zealand, to whom I owe a good deal both by way of positive criticism or advice and also through the assistance which they sometimes unconsciously gave me in revealing the misunderstandings and errors which are the most serious barriers in checking the acceptance of sound doctrine. My greatest debt is to Mr C. V. Janes, who was my colleague during 1934 in the Economic Department of the Bank of New South Wales in Sydney, and who subjected the whole of my manuscript to a careful, detailed criticism which enabled me to improve my work in many important respects. I have also to thank Mr H. D. Dickinson, of the University of Leeds, and Professor R. C. Mills, of the University of Sydney, who have read my manuscript and offered useful criticisms. Readers of the book are especially indebted to my wife, without whose persistent and tactful criticism my obscurities and harshnesses of style would have been still more numerous than they are.

ALLAN G. B. FISHER

UNIVERSITY OF OTAGO, DUNEDIN
May 15, 1935

CONTENTS

CHAPTER VI

CHAPTER VII

CHAPTER I

INTRODUCTION

AT the end of a long and active life, Alfred Marshall still found it impossible to complete the structure of his economic theory as he had intended with a volume to be called "Progress: Its Economic Conditions".[1] It would clearly be presumptuous for other economists to pretend that, at any stage of their career, they could convincingly expound "the high theme of economic progress",[2] a task which even Marshall had found too formidable. Nevertheless it seems to-day more urgent than ever to disseminate a wide understanding of the economic conditions and implications of progress; the rate of material progress which we are able to maintain is seriously diminished by widespread ignorance of the character of the changes and adjustments which it demands, and the disappointingly slow rate of recovery from the depression is in no small measure to be explained by this fact.

The concept of progress in general is one about which wide divergences of opinion are obviously possible. We need not, however, pause here to consider whether progress, interpreted in the light of some philosophic view of man and the universe, is either possible or desirable. We are here concerned with material progress only, with the increase and elabora-

---

[1] *Memorials of Alfred Marshall*, p. 65.
[2] *Principles of Economics*, p. 461.

1

tion of the goods and services whose production we are able to organise, and it is sufficient for our purposes that the objective conditions do exist upon which such material progress depends, and that a large proportion of the inhabitants of modern communities desires to enjoy the material progress which these conditions make possible. In these circumstances, it is an important part of the economist's task to depict as simply and as clearly as he can the nature of the changes, the adjustments and adaptations, which are needed for the realisation of the community's desires for further progress. Because he has so often neglected this task, the economist must himself bear much of the responsibility for the almost complete failure, which the late Professor Cannan has so energetically criticised,[1] to get across into the consciousness of the ordinary man an understanding of even the most elementary economic truths.

In spite of the work of more profound thinkers,[2] it is unfortunately true that these elementary truths have frequently been presented in the background of a static economy, the so-called Stationary State. It may well be that this method of approach is "the hallmark of second-rate economic thinking",[3] but there is no doubt that its influence has been important, and elementary truths which are presented in this way naturally fail to find a ready acceptance because in real life their application is inevitably combined with the application of another set of principles to be derived from observation of a growing, progressive economy. It is the

[1] "The Need for Simpler Economics", *Economic Journal*, September 1933.
[2] Cf. R. W. Souter, *Prolegomena to Relativity Economics*, especially ch. iv.
[3] *Ibid.* p. 15.

practical effect of this second set of principles which attracts the attention of the man in the street, and to their elucidation the economist who wishes to take a realistic view of his problems must devote much of his effort.[1]

Every problem of economic organisation would be much easier to solve if it presented itself in a society which was content with the standards of material welfare which had already been attained, and had no wish to improve them. The allocation of labour and capital into the various industries could then proceed along the lines which the experience of the past had already made familiar. There would be few unpredictable new factors to upset our calculations, and those who had already found a satisfactory opening for their labour or for the investment of their capital would seldom find themselves called upon to make new and unpleasant adjustments to changing conditions. Even if population continued to increase, the maintenance of capital accumulation at the same rate as that to which people with reasonably assured incomes had already become accustomed would be sufficient to prevent any serious problems of adaptation from arising.

There is much to be said for the type of society which would be based on such static economic foundations, and it need not be inconsistent with a high level of cultural activity. No reputable economist has ever maintained that material progress was an end, good in itself, for the sake of which everything else had to be sacrificed. But if economic progress were to cease today, we should find it necessary to submit to a rigid

[1] Cf. J. Åkerman, *Economic Progress and Economic Crises*, p. viii. Only when the formation of new means of production and development can be included in economic theory have we provided a bridge between economic process and economic reasoning.

and ossified social stratification, which is rightly abhorrent to large sections of modern public opinion. The conclusion that we should rest satisfied with existing income standards is one which people living in a capitalist society can scarcely be expected to accept; the gross inequalities of capitalist society, if they are to be justified at all, can find justification only in the belief that sufficient plasticity and flexibility are maintained to make possible a steady if irregular improvement in the standard of living, while at the same time opportunities are offered from time to time to individuals to transfer to departments of work where the level of remuneration is higher. The condemnation of considerable sections of the population for all time or for any long period to the low standards which for many people are all that can be expected if we are content with existing methods of production, is clearly inconsistent with this justification, and if such condemnation is believed to be necessary, the case for maintaining a capitalist organisation of society crumbles away. Most people, at any rate in Western countries, are anxious that the course of material progress, which has been so rapid during the last hundred years, should not now be checked. While in every country, even in normal times, there are so many people living in a state of poverty which makes it impossible to pay the slightest attention to anything not directly connected with the provision of elemental material needs, it would be unreasonable to check the further progress which would enable these sections of the population to enjoy a more varied mode of life, and cultivate social and cultural relationships more worthy of a true civilisation. It is worthy of note that the people who express doubts about the value of further material

progress are usually people who, even in these depressed
years, enjoy a considerable degree of comfort. It would
be a matter for regret if their hesitations were permanently to exclude large sections of the population
from the possibility of ever reaching similarly com-
fortable positions, and it is not easy to discuss patiently
with them their complacent relegation of other people
to permanently depressed standards of living. The time
may come when we may reasonably call a halt, satisfied that everybody everywhere has reasonable opportunities for living a civilised life, but that time is
clearly far distant.[1]

A large proportion of the inhabitants of modern
states, we have said, desires to enjoy the benefits of
material progress, but at the same time many of them
are equally devoted to other ends which conflict with
material progress. In fact, nearly all our economic
problems to-day either find their origin in, or at least
are made much more complicated by a widespread
confusion of mind, which leaves us unable to decide
how far material progress is to be made the sole or

---

[1] Cf. Robbins, *The Great Depression*, pp. 142-3: "The majority of
the human race are still very poor, and if, in the interests of a supposed
stability, a halt is to be called in the process of raising real incomes,
it is an issue which should be squarely presented to those who are most
affected by it. It is all very well for the dilettante economists of wealthy
universities, their tables groaning beneath a sufficiency of the good
things of this world, their garages furnished with private means of
transport, to say 'Food is cheap enough. Charabancs are vulgar. The
railways are admirable. We have enough of plenty. Let us safeguard
security.' It is for the millions to whom a slice of bacon more or less, or
a bus ride to the sea, still matter, to make the decision."

It is not easy to identify the "dilettante economists of wealthy universities" who are here attacked, the error of which they are alleged to be
guilty being in fact more characteristic of people who would regard it
almost as an insult to be called an economist. The error is, however,
very widespread and influential, and whoever is guilty of it, it merits
severe attack.

ultimate objective of economic policy or how far it should be sacrificed in the interests of individual security and stability. It is unfortunately not true that "we all know where we wish to go",[1] or it is at least true that many of us want to move simultaneously in opposite directions. One Government department takes considerable trouble and spends money in improving the standard of wheat production; at the same time another Government department takes care that the price of wheat shall be kept up, with the result that consumers are unable to get any benefit from scientific research into wheat. Many people applaud both activities, without observing that one is a direct contradiction of the other. If we want progress, it is reasonable to encourage more wheat research; if we want a static organisation, it is reasonable to keep wheat prices steady, but we cannot consistently aim at both ends at the same time.

A decision upon some of the issues which will emerge in this discussion would require indeed that we should look much deeper than mere material changes. The widespread confusion of mind to which we have referred is the expression of a fundamental and perennial conflict the ultimate resolution of which is likely to depend upon more than economic considerations.

In dealing with these issues, it has been said, "the economist must be a political philosopher and a political scientist as well as an economist: he must display constructive imagination and capacity for constructive 'political invention' in the development of improved institutional forms".[2] Whether it is reasonable or not to expect the economist to shoulder such

---

[1] O. W. M. Sprague, *Recovery and Common Sense*, p. 1.
[2] R. W. Souter, *op. cit.* p. 165.

heavy responsibilities, there is no question that the statesman whose undóubted duty it is to face these problems cannot afford to neglect any one of their aspects. At the same time it is important for all of us to have clear ideas about the changes which economic considerations would suggest, and about the consequences of neglecting them.

Material progress means change, and change frequently inflicts much inconvenience and suffering upon individuals directly affected; it is largely the fear of these inconveniences which prevents us from facing squarely and confidently the fundamental readjustments without which recovery from depression at a satisfactory level must be impossible. It is not surprising in a period where the risks associated with change are so overwhelming, that the opinion should be widespread that, "in these days, security of tenure seems to be the most important consideration". The modern world for the most part desires material progress, but with equal emphasis it also for the most part does not desire the changes without which material progress is impossible. If, however, at the same time as we insist on further material progress, we jib in consequence of our devotion to security at the readjustments which progress makes inevitable, we should not be surprised if the economic mechanism shows signs of breaking down.

The conflicts which arise are, as we shall see, to a large extent conflicts between the divergent interests of different sections of the community, or of different nations, or between the special interests of groups and the wider interests of the whole nation or of the whole world. The disintegrating effect of such conflicts is, however, all the more serious and insidious because there are also similar conflicts inside the mind of the statesman, the banker, the business man, the trade-union leader or the man in the street. Action has often been irresolute and futile, because of the irresolution and division in the minds of those responsible for advising and carrying it out. Often they have failed to make clear to themselves the ultimate ends towards which policy should be directed; uncertainty about ends means vacillation in action, and the endeavour to follow simultaneously paths which right from the outset point in opposite directions inevitably ends in catastrophe.

The fact of change is one which even the most elementary exposition of economic theory has never completely ignored. It is pointed out that time must be allowed in order that adaptation to changed conditions may become perfect, and further that this adaptation can seldom be complete, as before the process is finished, new changes requiring new adaptations are likely to occur in other parts of our organisation.

Apart, moreover, from the effects of new and independent causes of change, the process of adaptation itself is likely to generate conditions which make possible still further advances in productivity. "Every important advance in the organisation of production, regardless of whether it is based upon anything which, in a narrow or technical sense, would be called a new 'invention', or involves a fresh application of the fruits of scientific progress to industry, alters the conditions of industrial activity, and initiates responses elsewhere in the industrial structure which in turn have a further unsettling effect. Thus change becomes progressive and propagates itself in a cumulative way."[1] We have,

---

[1] Allyn Young, "Increasing Returns and Economic Progress", *Economic Journal*, December 1928, p. 533. Cf. R. W. Souter, *op. cit.* p. 32.

however, been inclined to think of change as in its nature unpredictable, and therefore unsuitable as a subject for scientific generalisation, and have accordingly made little effort to describe in general terms the changes which are likely to occur. It is nevertheless desirable that an effort should be made to develop a general theory of change, and especially of the changes which are associated with material progress. For though to a large extent it is true that the content of change is unpredictable, we can nevertheless state some useful truths about it, if we first make an important, though not perfectly watertight, distinction between two kinds of change which are likely to occur in any economy, changes on the side of demand, in consumers' tastes, in fashion, on the one hand, and, on the other, changes in the efficiency of production, affecting the supply of goods, and making possible or necessary a different level of material welfare. The one is often dependent upon and has its origin in the other. Motor-cars replace horses partly because they are more efficient, but also because they become more fashionable. Nevertheless the distinction is useful for practical purposes, and can be made without much risk of confusion. It is scarcely possible to say much about the real content of changes in taste ; even after the advertiser has done his best it is notoriously impossible to predict or to control the whims of fashion. Changes in taste or fashion, transfers of demand, whatever their content, whether from Eastern to Western modes of dress, from bull-baiting and cock-fighting to cinemas and vaudeville, or from feather boas to fur stoles, will necessitate a corresponding remodelling of our economy on the production side. People will have to give up raising ostriches and turn their attention instead to hunting seals and foxes.

The real content of the changes on the supply side, making possible more efficient production, is also largely unpredictable. We cannot easily tell beforehand whether the next important advance in science will affect the production of wheat, of woollen fabrics, of aeroplane engines, or of calculating machines. But we can predict in general terms—and it is here that scientific treatment of the economic implications of change becomes possible—the consequences for the general structure of our economy, wherever these improvements may happen to be applied.[1] If we allow the economic organism to make the proper response, such improvements make possible higher average income levels, and although the expenditure of individuals may be unpredictable, we can describe without serious risk of error the character of the new demand for goods and services which will be forthcoming when large groups of people find themselves able to enjoy higher average incomes. In order that this new demand may be effective, corresponding changes must be made in the structure of the productive organisation, and further important generalisations are possible about the consequences which will ensue if we refuse to make these changes or are unduly dilatory in carrying them to completion. The changes are not unlike those which variations in taste require, but the adjustments which they demand are more fundamental, and they exhibit a uniformity of direction which makes them suitable subjects for scientific

---

[1] Pigou (*Industrial Fluctuations*, p. 53) distinguishes between "net changes" in taste and changes which cancel out, but the former are impossible unless the volume of production changes at the same time.

investigation. In our survey of the economic implications of material progress, we shall attempt such a scientific investigation.

Without pretending to make any profound analysis of the minutiae of abstract economic theory,[1] it is important therefore to attempt some outline of the changes which material progress demands, and to indicate at the same time the nature of the obstacles which frequently stand in the way of their realisation, and the consequences of failure to surmount these obstacles.

It has become a commonplace in modern discussions of economic policy that it is necessary to maintain an appropriate "balance" between different kinds of production. It has not been equally widely understood that the balance which it is desirable to maintain must in a progressive economy be constantly undergoing change, that the balance which was appropriate in 1905 or 1915 or 1925 will certainly be inappropriate in 1935, and that any effort in 1935 to restore the balance which was appropriate at some earlier year will end in dislocation and instability. But what does a change in the character of the balance between different kinds of production mean, in terms of the lives of individual workers and investors? As a rule it must mean important changes in the character of the work which they find desirable to offer the community, and equally important changes in the directions towards which it is desirable to guide the flow of capital.

The kernel of the economic problem of material progress is indeed this constant necessity for change on the part of members of modern industrial communities, the necessity for change of work, and the

[1] For some penetrating observations on this theme from the point of view of methodology, see R. W. Souter, *Prolegomena to Relativity Economics.*

necessity for change in the character of investment. Unfortunately a real understanding of the kind of change which becomes necessary has frequently been hampered by the widespread habit of describing the situation in vague general terms which mean next to nothing. There has been much discussion during the depression, for example, about the necessity for " re-adjustment" ; it is difficult, however, to avoid the con-clusion that readjustment has been little more than a "blessed" word, designed to give comfort to the man who uses it, rather than to shed light upon the com-plexities of an unprecedentedly difficult situation. A clear understanding of the meaning of readjustment has seldom been possible because it has not been realised that it is inevitably associated in the closest way with the necessity for changing one's occupation or the character of one's investments.

Our main task is to outline the readjustments which material progress demands, and then to consider the more important factors which, in the modern world, make such readjustment so difficult. In so doing we shall get some insight into the funda-mental contradictions which endanger social stability to-day. We shall at the same time be directing atten-tion to some of the most important causes of the per-sistence of depression, and explaining at least in part the paradox of "poverty amid plenty," which in the twentieth century appears so tragically absurd. We cannot comfort ourselves with the belief that failure to make the necessary adjustments merely checks the rate of material progress. It also threatens to destroy the advances which have already been made, and if it does not explain fully the coming of the depression, it goes far in explaining the tardiness of the recovery.

CHAPTER II

MATERIAL PROGRESS AND CHANGES IN THE DEMAND FOR GOODS

MATERIAL progress is identical with a raising of the average standard of real income.[1] Unless average real incomes rise, there is no material progress, though there may be important elements of progress of other and profounder kinds. A study of the economics of a materially progressive society must therefore include a study of the adjustments in the organisation of production which are necessary in the face of a rising average income - level. The two processes, rising incomes and changing production organisation, are not independent processes. We do not increase incomes first and adapt our methods of production afterwards. Rather at the same time as we improve

[1] An exhaustive analysis here would demand some consideration of changes in income distribution which occurred either independently of, or at the same time as, changes in the average. This subject has been deliberately excluded, except so far as changes in relative income are themselves a probable consequence of the adaptations in production which are our main theme. The subject is excluded not because it is unimportant, but because it is desirable, in the interests of clear thinking, to confine our attention to the adaptations which should follow improvements in the efficiency of production and which therefore will tend to raise the average income level. It is, however, also implicit in our argument that those adaptations are themselves likely to diminish the existing inequality of income distribution (cf. pp. 65-7). The measurement and comparison of real income is a task beset with grave difficulties, but it is believed that the idea of a rising average level of real income will be sufficiently clear to justify us in dispensing with any further analysis of these difficulties.

our production, the average level of real income also rises.[1] From the side of the consumer, we can describe the material progress of the nineteenth century by saying that the average man had a larger income at the end of it than his great-grandfather had at its beginning; from the side of the producer, we can say that throughout the century new industries were steadily developing which absorbed a steadily growing proportion of the world's labour and capital, so that a relatively smaller proportion was left (and was needed) for the older staple industries. Nevertheless, it is convenient for many purposes to study the two processes separately, with a view later to insisting on the intimate nature of the relation which must bind them together.

The possible causes of growth of wealth, of improvements in productive capacity, are well known; there has probably been too much insistence in this connection on hard work and thrift, though these no doubt are essential. The standards of wealth in many backward countries are low because of the general inefficiency of work, and to become wealthier the inhabitants of these countries might be urged to work harder, or more regularly, as for example has been done in Russia. If people were more thrifty, standards of wealth would

---

[1] This is one of the frequent instances where confusion sometimes arises on account of a careless transition from modes of speech which are appropriate to individuals to apparently similar modes of speech which are quite inappropriate when applied to an economy. It is quite sensible for an individual to think of getting his increase of income first and then looking about for some way of spending it; but this method of approach, if applied to a whole economy, is quite meaningless. A community cannot increase its income first, and afterwards set to work to produce the things on which the increased income can be spent. The two processes of getting an increased income and producing new things are, for a community, identical. Unless the new things are produced, there is no increase of income.

also no doubt rise; but great thriftiness has been at least as often an effect as a cause of increased production, and it is probably more important in practice now to devise machinery to check the waste of savings than to make any strenuous efforts to increase their volume. Useful advances might also be made if people were trained to make better use of, and have a more discriminating appreciation for, the incomes at their disposal. In the past, however, a more important cause of material progress has been the discovery of new resources. The material progress of Europe in the sixteenth and seventeenth centuries, for example, was largely the consequence of the discovery of America. Unquestionably, however, the factor which historically has been most important, and whose importance is certain to be even greater in the future, is the growth of knowledge.[1] We soon reach a limit beyond which the vigour and keenness of our work and the accumulations of our thrift cannot be pushed; the limits to the discovery of new natural resources are also clearly defined, but no limits can be set to the expansion of knowledge, either in the natural and social sciences or in their technical applications or in the field of organisation and administration. Our task, then, is to trace out the adjustments in the organisation of production which growth of knowledge makes necessary if the community's needs are to be satisfied in the more adequate way which growth of knowledge should make possible.

If we analyse the expenditure of people with rising incomes, we can readily see that the distribution of employment is likely to have a fairly close relationship to the proportions in which consumers spend money

[1] Cannan, *Wealth*, p. 19.

on different kinds of commodity. If we know, for example, that the average inhabitant of northern China is estimated to spend about 60 per cent of his income on food,[1] while the average inhabitant of Australia spends much less, we shall not be surprised to learn that, in spite of the complications introduced by external trade and the export of foodstuffs, the proportion of the Chinese population engaged in agricultural and similar pursuits is much greater than the proportion of the Australian population similarly employed. We can see also that the importance of any industry as a field of employment in 1935 will be relatively much less than it was thirty years ago, if it can be shown that the proportion of consumers' expenditure devoted to the products of that industry has declined. Rising income-levels will always mean, are in fact the same thing as, changes in the relative importance of different kinds of production.

This is, at bottom, merely another way of saying that the processes of production and the processes of consumption must always be organically linked together in the closest possible way. No one has ever been stupid enough formally to deny this connection, but even intelligent people often act in a way which implies such a denial. It is often argued, for example, that work of a certain type, or in a certain place, should be provided without seriously considering whether the products of such work are likely to be wanted by anyone. Among the reasons which induce Mr F. Gisborne to desire more extensive land settlement in Australia is "the tranquillising influence exercised by a power rural class on the social and political

---

[1] L. K. Tao, "Food Consumption in the Chinese Standard of Living", *Problems of the Pacific*, 1931, p. 53.

condition of a country. . . . Such a class is much needed in Australia at the present time to check the mischievous vagaries of city mobs. . . . The existence of huge cities abounding with combustible material for the use of social incendiaries is a continual menace to the safety of a country." [1] In determining which occupations ought to be encouraged, that is to say, we are told that we should ask not whether the things produced are likely to be wanted, but whether their production will encourage a political and social outlook of a particular colour. When policy is directed in this way towards the attainment of non-economic ends without paying due regard to the economic losses which will be involved, it is worth while to insist with some emphasis on the close relation which there should always be between consumption and production. With this guiding principle in mind, it is a useful exercise to attempt to sketch out the things which members of a community would buy as they became wealthier, and then to consider how these things can be produced in the right quantities and in the proper order.

Before our analysis is concluded, it will be necessary to say something about the efficiency of the organisation whereby the necessary adjustments are to be made, but in the first instance such problems of organisation can be neglected as being irrelevant. The fundamental principles which need to be emphasised are equally important, whether the structure of our society is to be capitalist, communist or anything else. Both communist dictators and capitalist entrepreneurs must pay attention to the principles here outlined, if the possi-

[1] "Urbanisation and Land Settlement", *Australian Quarterly*, December 1933, pp. 118-19. Cf. "The Urbanisation Peril in Australia", *ibid.* December 1932.

bilities of material progress are to be converted into actualities, and if chronic dislocation is to be avoided. The methods of organisation adopted under these conditions by the two types of society would be different, but the basic character of the changes required must be identical. In visualising the things which are likely to be purchased as incomes rise, we may think first in terms of the expenditure of an individual, perhaps of ourselves; individual habits of expenditure, however, are varied, and it is probably better to think in terms of the expenditure of groups within which the effects of individual differences will tend to cancel out. Much statistical work dealing with consumption has been done since the days of Engel (1857) or earlier, and many household budget studies have been undertaken for a wide variety of purposes. The aspect of those studies which is of importance here is the light which is thrown upon the varying ratios of expenditure upon different classes of goods at varying income-levels. It has commonly been stated that Engel laid down definite laws of consumption which were derived from his analysis of household budget expenditure. As the income of a family increases, a smaller percentage, he is said to have maintained, is spent on food, the percentage of expenditure on clothing remains approximately the same, the percentage for rent, fuel, and light is exactly the same, while a constantly increasing percentage is expended on education, health, recreation, amusement and other miscellaneous items. Engel himself was apparently not responsible for these detailed "laws".[1] More extensive enquiries have

[1] C. C. Zimmerman, "Ernst Engel's Law of Expenditures", *Quarterly Journal of Economics*, November 1932.

shown wider variations in expenditure on clothing and
housing, but have to a considerable extent confirmed
Engel's conclusions about expenditure on food and on
miscellaneous items. Engel's own calculations were as
follows:

Object of Expenditure	Percentage Division of Annual Family Income (1857) in Saxony of—		
	£70	£90	£150
Food . . .	62 ⎫	55 ⎫	50 ⎫
Shelter . . .	12 ⎬ 95	12 ⎬ 90	12 ⎬
Clothing . . .	16 ⎪	18 ⎪	18 ⎪
Fuel and light . .	5 ⎭	5 ⎭	5 ⎭
Education . . .	2 ⎫	3·5 ⎫	5·5 ⎫
Public security . .	1 ⎬ 5	2 ⎬ 10	3 ⎬ 15
Health . . .	1 ⎪	2 ⎪	3 ⎪
Comfort and service .	1 ⎭	2·5 ⎭	3·5 ⎭
	100	100	100

These income-levels are very low, but American
studies have given similar results for higher ranges of
income.

PERCENTAGE DISTRIBUTION OF EXPENDITURE AT DIFFERENT
INCOME-LEVELS BY FAMILIES IN THE UNITED STATES,
1918–19

Income	Food	Rent	Clothing	Fuel and Light	Furniture and Furnishings	Miscel-laneous
Under £180	44·1	14·5	13·2	6·8	3·5	17·8
£180–£240	42·4	13·9	14·5	6·0	4·4	18·7
£240–£300	39·6	13·8	15·9	5·6	4·8	20·2
£300–£360	37·2	13·5	16·7	5·2	5·5	21·8
£360–£420	35·7	13·2	17·5	5·0	5·5	23·0
£420–£500	34·6	12·1	18·7	4·5	5·7	24·3
£500 and Over	34·9	10·6	20·4	4·1	5·4	24·7

An estimate for higher income groups in the United States adopts a somewhat different basis for classification.

Income	Food for Family, including Servants	Housing	Clothing	Fuel and Light	Wages of Servants	Automobiles and Yachts	Miscellaneous
£1,000	27·2	18·0	14·3	3·3	4·5	9·2	23·5
£2,000	19·2	18·3	11·9	3·2	9·5	9·8	28·1
£3,000	15·8	18·6	10·3	3·0	11·5	10·0	30·8
£4,000	13·7	18·9	9·3	2·8	12·3	10·0	33·0
£5,000	12·0	19·2	8·7	2·6	12·7	10·0	34·8
£6,000	10·4	19·5	8·1	2·4	12·9	10·0	36·7
£7,000	9·1	19·8	7·6	2·2	13·1	10·0	38·2
£8,000	7·9	20·1	7·1	2·1	13·3	10·0	39·5
£9,000	6·9	20·4	6·7	1·9	13·5	10·0	40·6
£10,000	6·1	20·7	6·4	1·8	13·7	10·0	41·3

An examination of expenditure on food by groups of wage-earners in different European countries also gives a similar result.

VARIATION IN PROPORTION OF INCOME USED FOR FOOD IN DIFFERENT INCOME GROUPS IN THE UNITED KINGDOM, GERMANY, FRANCE AND BELGIUM, 1904–9

Weekly Income	United Kingdom	Germany	France	Belgium
Under 20s.	..	68·7	62·7	66·1
20s. to 25s.	67·5	64·5	60·8	64·8
25s. to 30s.	66·1	62·5	58·6	63·6
30s. to 35s.	65·2	59·2	57·9	62·1
35s. to 40s.	61·6	57·7	56·1	61·2
Over 40s.	57·1	56·3	52·8	57·0

The percentages recorded in China are different, but the general trend is the same.

DISTRIBUTION OF EXPENDITURE OF 100 CHINESE FAMILIES

Total Expenditure	Food	Rent	Clothing	Fuel and Light	Miscellaneous
£10–£14	76·9	9·0	5·1	7·6	1·4
£14–£18	80·3	7·9	4·3	5·6	1·9
£18–£22	78·0	8·0	5·9	5·8	2·2
£22–£26	72·7	7·6	9·0	7·5	3·1
£26–£30	72·4	7·3	8·9	7·3	4·1
£30 and over	72·0	6·8	9·8	5·7	5·6

The relatively low expenditure on food by the lowest expenditure group here is probably to be explained in part by the small size of the families which were included in that group.[1]

The figures which have here been quoted by way of illustration, and to which numerous additions might easily have been made, have been collected by widely different methods and at widely varying points of time. It would be unsafe to assume literal accuracy in every detail, and in certain circumstances the general trend changes in some respects;[2] the general impression which the tables leave is, however, quite clear, and is in fact exactly what might have been expected from general observation of our own habits of expenditure and the habits of other people about us. As income rises, the proportions spent on food and on fuel and light steadily diminish, and the proportion spent on miscellaneous items increases. The trend in respect of rent is first downward, but then tends to rise again, while the trend in clothing expenditure is exactly the opposite of this. If our income is very small, we must

[1] All the tables quoted are from Waite, *Economics of Consumption*, ch. ix. Cf. Berridge, Winslow and Flinn, *Purchasing Power of Consumer*, Book II. chs. iii., iv.

[2] Cf. Zimmerman, *loc. cit.*

spend it all on essential foodstuffs, simple articles of clothing, low-grade housing. As our income rises we can afford to purchase food and clothing of better quality, but we also spend more on furniture and household gear, on newspapers and books, and with further increases, the items on which we spend money become still more varied, including travel and transport facilities, amusements, and various cultural interests. Engel indeed maintained that at the "normal" level of welfare, people would spend a maximum of 80 per cent of their income for the "reasonable" satisfaction of material needs with the remainder reserved for "higher" cultural needs. But any attempt to define a "normal" level of welfare in these terms means the adoption of that static point of view which we are here concerned to reject. The important and obvious fact is that whatever level of welfare has been reached, any improvement in it will mean a constant tendency to increase expenditure on certain items at a more rapid rate than the rate of increase of income as a whole, as well as to buy some things which previously were not available at all.

Incidentally some of the new things will in part displace some of the old. A man who buys a motor-car will spend less on tram fares, and he may also economise in his expenditure on clothing; in addition the character of expenditure within each group—food, clothing or the like—will also change. There will be more scope for variations in individual taste, and important changes in the quality of the products purchased. As income increases, we can afford to be a little more exigent in our demand for variety and extensiveness in the stocks carried by retail shops, we can more readily purchase goods which have been transported over long distances, or we prefer to buy goods packed in neat or even beautiful boxes or tins. Where our fathers bought food and clothing, we can insist on buying food plus artistic packages, clothing plus delivery at the door and all the other conveniences of a highly organised retail establishment.

In practice it is certainly often difficult to distinguish between extensions of retail trade and commercial activity which truly correspond to the growing complexity of the real demands of a community whose income is rising, and extensions which are wasteful. It is often too easy to start business as a small shopkeeper or a commission agent, and this very fact attracts into such work many people who find later that they are not needed there and incidentally lose a considerable part of such capital resources as they have been able to command. But in criticising the wastefulness of a great deal of modern commercial activity, it is important to bear in mind that even if such waste were eliminated, there would be a tendency for the proportion of the population engaged in commercial work to increase as economic life became more complex.

What is true if we survey the expenditure habits of people at different income-levels at the same point of time must be equally true of the expenditure habits of groups whose average income-level, for any reason, rises from time to time. The differences in the relative importance of the various items of expenditure will then correspond fairly closely to the differences already observed at the different income-levels. The problem of production is always the problem of allocating resources in such a way as to ensure supplies in the correct proportions of the various things which people will wish to purchase, and when the average income-level rises, the problem of production therefore becomes the problem of changing the previous allocation, in conformity with the changes in the relative importance of items of expenditure. If the change is not made, the rising average income-level for which the essential conditions are already in existence will be impossible. The application of Engel's laws to the successive stages of a progressive economy gives a rough picture of the changes in the structure of production which are essential if the potentialities of material progress are to be realised.

Any addition to the stock of knowledge will impose upon a communist dictator the duty of redistributing the supplies of labour and other resources under his control. In deciding how much of anything it is desirable to produce, he must take care that he does not allocate so much labour and capital for that purpose that there is insufficient left for the production of other things which on the whole the community is likely to value more. This may mean, in fact in many cases is almost certain to mean, production of a smaller quantity of some things than is ideally desirable. In a poor community, the supply of boots might be defective. "I do not produce more boots," says the Dictator, "because if I did, houses would be even worse than they are." As productive capacity improved, the Dictator would also change the character of the labour in some industries. Up to a certain point he would probably introduce a little additional labour into all the industries which were already established, but the supplies of labour would be increased at widely varying rates, and as some industries might, quite soon, find themselves adequately equipped to meet all the requirements of the community, he might also, if he did not regard the claims of leisure as paramount, open up a few entirely new industries. Whenever it was found possible to supply the need for any commodity by the labours of a diminished number of people, there would be general rejoicing, and the surplus formerly employed in that industry would be drafted elsewhere to produce other things, apparently not so important, but perhaps more interesting, which the community had previously lacked.

Though we cannot predict in detail the nature of the new goods and services which a community with rising income-standards will wish to purchase, observation of the expenditure habits of people who are already wealthy, aided by general reasoning, enables us to make some safe generalisations about what is likely to occur when poor communities find that they can spend more than they have been in the habit of spending in the past. In seeking for such generalisations, it will be convenient to suggest a bird's-eye view of world economic history, in three main stages, which will assist us to distinguish in broad outline the character of the changes which increased wealth demands. The form in which this sketch is cast is suggested by the habit of speech familiar in Australia and in New Zealand, where a distinction is commonly drawn between primary producers, including farmers, fishermen, people engaged in forestry, and sometimes miners, and secondary producers, who for the most part are engaged in manufactures.

(i) In the primary producing stage, a stage beyond which large areas of the world have not yet passed, agricultural and pastoral occupations were the most important. Many important improvements in production technique took place during this period, but the Malthusian population pressure was usually a real thing and increases in food supply were eagerly desired on account of the constant dread of famine. The improvements also were slow, science was primitive, people were poor, and it was difficult to get capital for trying out new ideas. There were in the aggregate numerous transfers of labour to other and new types of industry, and even during this period there were difficulties and complaints about the hardships which such transfers involved; during the Tudor period Sir Thomas More complained that "sheep have become devourers of men",[1] and similar complaints about the displacement of labour were made in 1673 against the introduction of the stage-coach.[2]

(ii) In the manufacturing or industrial or secondary producing stage, agriculture became relatively less important, and the production of textiles, of iron and steel products and of other manufactured goods offered rapidly widening opportunities for employment and investment. It is not possible to give definite dates, but Great Britain was obviously entering this stage by the end of the eighteenth century. Some countries seem not to have entered it yet, but distinctions between countries are now of little consequence from the standpoint of this analysis, as improvements in transport and communication ensure that the effects of other improvements in any single country are felt everywhere. During this period there have been enormous increases in productivity, due mainly to extensions of knowledge relating both to agricultural and to other types of pro-

---

[1] Lipson, *Economic History of England*, i. p. 142.

[2] Sir Josiah Stamp, "Must Science ruin Economic Progress?" *Hibbert Journal*, April 1934, pp. 387-93.

duction. The increases in capital which were also essential have been the result as much as the cause of increased production. Population has continued to grow; it grew in fact more rapidly than ever before and this eased the problem of transfer, for food standards during the first period were often very low, and it was therefore natural that a large proportion of the increases in income should be spent on more and better food. Some of the transfers during the second period were, however, extensive enough to cause great difficulty. Writers like Goldsmith deplored the depopulation of rural villages, and later there were agitations for the protection of English farmers against the competition of the much cheaper wheat produced in America and elsewhere overseas. There were transfers not only into manufacturing industries but also into types of work which had not hitherto been held in very high esteem as parts of the economic organisation, for example, travel, amusements, literature, etc. It is probable that these miscellaneous types of work had relatively more importance in the first stage than in the second, partly because many of them did not demand much capital and could therefore be more easily produced than goods which needed elaborate capital equipment which was impossible when savings were small. With growth of population, however, it became easier to recognise the importance of these types of work. Another characteristic feature of the transfers of labour during this period was the rapid growth of agricultural and pastoral population in "new" countries. It was desirable to have a rapidly growing population there to feed the rapidly growing industrial population of the older lands. Displacement in fact took place from both ends. More efficient factory production drove artisans accustomed to old methods of work abroad to develop the New World, and more efficient farming drove British farmers into industry at home. These transfers were greatly eased by the absence of restrictions on migration and the existence of comparatively low tariffs.

(iii) The "tertiary" stage begins in the twentieth century. In the popular phrase the problems of production in manufacturing seem now to have been solved; it becomes possible to divert an increasing proportion of human time and effort and of capital equipment into the production of goods and services, which do not fall readily, in the ordinary sense of the word, into either of the categories of primary or secondary production, and which are scarcely ever included in statistics of foreign trade, namely, facilities for travel, amusements of various kinds, governmental and other personal and intangible services, flowers, music, art, literature, education, science, philosophy and the like. These things, we have seen, were not unknown in either the primary or the secondary stage. Many indeed involve labour of the kind which Adam Smith described as unproductive because "it does not fix or realise itself in any permanent subject which endures after that labour is past",[1] and on that account people often looked down upon them as being of inferior status. When certain standards of efficiency in primary and secondary production have been reached, however, it is desirable that Adam Smith's "unproductive" services should occupy a rapidly increasing proportion of the time of the community. It is the growing importance of these services which characterises the tertiary stage. "Those countries which have the highest standards of life

---

[1] *Wealth of Nations*, Book II, ch. iii.

ought to be those employing the largest proportion of their populations in the supply of 'luxuries'. All that stands in the way are economic and ethical standards no longer appropriate to the tendencies at work." [1] The enjoyment of these services further presupposes an increasing amount of leisure, and it is characteristic of the "tertiary" period that leisure has in fact played an increasingly important part in the life of the ordinary man. Since the beginning of this century, there have been widespread reductions in working hours, which correspond closely to the normal evolution of industry. The pressing problem of adjustment in the fourth decade of the twentieth century is the problem of reorganising the structure of production so that the transfer of resources to the production of these "tertiary" products, both goods and services, may be made as smoothly as possible. Insistence on the importance of these considerations does not mean that "the economic life of the world is being confronted by novel, vast and mysterious problems of a kind hitherto unknown. The problems involved are indeed of the utmost importance, but when their character is analysed, it will be found that they derive their importance more from a change of scale than from the novelty of their nature." [2] The discovery of solutions is, however, made much more difficult by the fact that our habits of thought are still often moulded by considerations more appropriate to the conditions of the second period and to some extent of the first.

It has been a well-known feature of modern economic development that the proportion of total population engaged in "tertiary" production has been

---

[1] T. E. Gregory, *Economic Journal*, December 1930, p. 566.
[2] T. E. Gregory, *Gold, Unemployment and Capitalism*, p. 245.

rapidly growing. The occupational records revealed by census investigations show a similar trend everywhere. It is estimated that in the United States from 1920 to 1927 the number of persons employed in agriculture declined by 860,000, and in manufacturing by 600,000, but during the same period the number in the public services increased by 100,000, in construction work by 600,000, in transport and communication by nearly a million, in mercantile employment by 1,400,000, and in miscellaneous occupations in hotels, restaurants, garages, repair shops, moving-picture places, barber shops, hospitals, insurance work, professional offices and the like, by more than $2\frac{1}{2}$ millions.[1] Even during the depression the same trend has been observed in Great Britain. "Between 1923 and 1933, the number of persons employed in manufacturing remained about the same, and the number employed in mining and quarrying fell from 1,267,150 to 715,120. Meanwhile the number employed in transport and distribution rose from 1,812,930 to 2,442,640 and in miscellaneous services from 481,430 to 704,710." [2] According to the census figures of gainfully occupied persons, the number of persons attached to agriculture declined between 1920 and 1930 by 193,814. The number attached to manufacturing increased by 1,278,773 or 10 per cent; transport and communication, by 746,318 or 24·4 per cent; trade, 1,823,783 or 42·8 per cent; public service, 117,680 or 15·9 per cent; professional service, 1,082,733 or 49 per cent; domestic and personal service, 1,572,456 or 46·5 per cent; clerical, 913,488 or 29·4 per cent; "practically the

[1] *Recent Economic Changes*, vol. ii. pp. 877-8. For similar and more detailed figures covering the period 1870–1930, see R. G. Hurlin and M. B. Givens, *Recent Social Trends*, ch. vi.

[2] *Economist*, June 28, 1934, p. 914.

whole of the 7,000,000 increase in population was absorbed into transport, trade, professional service and domestic and personal service".

Sir Frederick G. Hopkins, president of the British Association, pointed out at the Leicester meeting on September 6, 1933, that "from eight to ten individuals in the world are now engaged on scientific research for every one so engaged twenty years ago". Such a change as this is clearly an indication of progress, and in the same way no sensible person complains because the proportion of teachers to total population is now much higher than it used to be. The transfers are being made, but they are not being made with sufficient speed, and they are made in the face of widespread feeling that the new types of work are wasteful and unproductive. If our argument is sound, poetry and philosophy are significant not only on account of their own intrinsic value, but also because their organisation on an economic basis is an essential condition for stability in a progressive economy. A progressive economy must be chronically unstable unless there is a steady and continuous flow of resources into types of economic activity which a less wealthy economy has been unable to afford. It is essential that steadily increasing attention should be paid to the production of the amenities of life, of things which poorer communities have been in the habit of regarding as luxuries.

The importance which it is proper to attach to the development of "tertiary" industries as a means for diminishing unemployment is not to be measured merely by a calculation of the number of people whom it is possible directly to employ in these fields. This number may be quite small in comparison with the total number unemployed at any given point of time. Nevertheless it is employment of this kind which deserves our first attention, for it is by appropriate action here that we are most likely to be able to introduce flexibility into the structure of production as a whole and provide opportunities for further expansion of employment in other fields as well.

We should not ignore the fact that in encouraging the growth of "tertiary" occupations it is extremely easy to select the wrong ones. Broadly speaking, our argument is in favour of a relatively rapid extension of "luxury" trades and industries. But the fact that some expansion, indeed even a rapid expansion of luxury trades, is desirable should not lead us to forget that certain luxury trades can easily be over-developed.

In general, the material progress, which growth of knowledge makes possible, necessitates the transfer of labour and of capital from such industries as the advance of knowledge has made more efficient into other, and, in many instances, entirely new industries. As the old staple industries find it increasingly easy to meet all the demands of a community growing in wealth, it is both desirable and necessary that there should be a comparative slackening in the rate of growth of these industries, a comparative acceleration in the rate of growth of other industries. As food supply becomes more adequate, it becomes possible to develop manufacturing more rapidly, and later, when supplies of manufactured goods also are abundant, the field which calls for most rapid development is the field of "tertiary" production. Unless these transfers are made, the conditions which make material progress possible are rendered ineffective, and confer no advantage upon anybody. On the contrary, they will cause dislocation and the delusive appearance of over-production. The complications of international trade will affect the relative importance of primary, secondary and "tertiary" production in different countries, but will in no way diminish the applicability of the general trend here described to every type of national economy. So long as the objective conditions for material progress are present, there will always be a tendency for the relative importance of primary production to diminish, and the relative importance of "tertiary" production to increase.

The paradox of poverty in a world of potential plenty, which has been used in support of the most divergent practical policies, is in part to be explained by our failure to appreciate the necessity for continuous changes and transfers of the kind described above. Potential plenty is the natural consequence of scientific advance; but we cannot enjoy the benefits of plenty unless we organise the productive capacity which has been released, so that it can be applied to the production of new things hitherto little known or even entirely unknown. If we refuse to do this, we are likely to find ourselves in the curious situation where not only are we deprived of the possibility of enjoying these new things, but some of us are also deprived of the possibility of enjoying, except by way of charity, the goods and services which are already abundantly supplied.

Most communities to-day very wisely spend large sums of money in encouraging scientific research of all kinds, and it has become a commonplace to dilate upon the wonders of modern science. But how can the fruits of scientific advance become available to the ordinary consumer who has money to spend? Clearly they will be useless to him unless they make possible the supply of goods and services at lower prices, and they will be attractive and advantageous to him in proportion as the lower prices release part of his income for expenditure along other lines. Unless some part of the productive forces, the labour and capital, which were formerly applied to the production of the articles which scientific advance now makes it possible to produce with a smaller expenditure of effort, is transferred to relatively new industries, there will be no new things for the consumer to buy.

The most obvious illustrations of material progress in the past are likely to be cast in terms of goods which were quite unknown to our ancestors, of radio sets and motor-cars, of electricity and gramophones. It is true that some notable periods of boom industrial activity have been inaugurated by the exploitation of new discoveries of this kind, but it would be a mistake to think exclusively in such terms. To do so would unduly encourage the tendency, already too strong, to adopt the Micawberish policy of waiting for something to turn up. Even if there are no new goods or services whatever, we can still visualise clearly the course of production in a progressing economy if we ask ourselves what things are likely to be purchased by people who find that their income is increasing. We do not need to wait for some complete novelty to be discovered; we can advance a long way merely by producing more of the things which are already well known but which at present only people with incomes well above the average can afford to purchase.

It should be needless to set down in specific terms the fact that the claim that some transfer of resources is necessary does not mean that any of the industries from which it is desirable to divert capital and labour should disappear altogether. It is entirely a question of rates of relative growth. The reactions in some quarters to proposals for retarding the rate of growth of agricultural and pastoral industries in countries which have hitherto made these the main fields of their economic activity suggest, however, that it may not be entirely superfluous to insist upon this obvious point.

We must certainly be prepared for drastic changes in our traditional outlook towards those industries which we are in the habit of describing as "basic". Because the history of England during the last century has been closely associated with the development of certain important export industries, because Australia's and New Zealand's prosperity is, as we say, "bound up" with primary production, we are inclined to think in times of depression that the first essential is to strengthen the export industries, or the industries associated with primary production. By strengthening these industries, we usually mean persuading more people to work and invest capital in them. If, however, our present difficulties are partly the result of the over-development of the basic industries, the proper line to follow is clearly the exact opposite of what is commonly suggested. The necessary "strengthening" of the traditional industries will be impossible unless we get more capital and more labour into industries which we have been in the habit of regarding as quite insignificant.

When we begin to reflect upon the products which people with rising real incomes are likely to purchase, many critics of fastidious taste, finding the objects of popular demand displeasing to their own finer sensibilities, are apt to conclude that it is undesirable that people should be encouraged to produce and purchase these things and are therefore inclined to throw overboard the whole of the argument which has here been set out. Apart from the fact that such an attitude confuses economic and non-economic standards of judgment, two other important considerations are relevant. If tastes are vulgar or debased, there is obviously nothing to be said against efforts to educate and refine them. To some slight degree this process is no doubt always going on, and no analysis of the implications of material progress can ever suggest that it is undesirable. Further, to conclude that, because people may produce certain things which we think consumers ought not to want, they should therefore be encouraged or compelled to produce other things which we are quite certain consumers do not want, for the very good reason that they already have quite enough, is a complete *non sequitur*. It may be regrettable that people "waste" their money on the movies or on cheap cosmetics or patent medicines or on something else which the critic happens to dislike, but it is no remedy for such a state of affairs to insist that more people should be induced to grow wheat, or some other staple commodity, which is already over-supplied.

There is perhaps some little justification for the alarms which are sometimes expressed about the dangers of excessive leisure. Many people at all income-levels simply do not know what to do with their spare time, with the result that all sorts of futile activities are encouraged from the practice of which other people are then able to make a living. This evil will not, however, be removed by endeavouring to persuade people to abandon profitable work of this kind and go back to agriculture or some other "basic" industry. It can be removed only by educating the public taste to appreciate and therefore to demand and be willing to pay for amusements and satisfactions of a higher and more genuinely civilised character. Nor does our argument compel us to deny that people sometimes spend their surplus income wastefully and extravagantly, or that, in order to keep up with the fashions of the day, they may at times unduly diminish their expenditure on more essential things. It cannot, however, be maintained that this practice is sufficiently general to justify the rejection of the view that the relatively rapid growth in recent years of the luxury or quasi-luxury trades is a reliable indication of expanding social wealth, and not merely the result of wasteful and undesirable transfer of demand from staple products to less necessary things. The movement may have been exaggerated in certain directions — there was some evidence immediately after the War to support this view [1]—but on the whole we spend more than our fathers and grandfathers did on "unnecessary" things because we can afford to do so.

In considering the prospects of economic development, especially in "new" countries, it is natural that in the early stages attention should be concentrated almost exclusively upon the discovery and exploitation of natural resources. When comparatively high standards of wealth, however, have been reached, this exclusive attention to natural resources is likely to distort our judgment when we have to select new fields for investment. Instead of thinking in terms of natural resources, our judgment will be more reliable if we

[1] A. L. Bowley, *Economic Consequences of the Great War*, p. 91.

think in terms of new wants, of what people with growing real incomes are likely to wish to purchase. The two methods of approach are not inconsistent. The prices which influence our scales of relative valuation are closely associated with costs of production, and costs of production themselves depend to a great extent on the relative scarcity of natural resources. In arranging a community's wants in order of importance, we can never afford to ignore the limitations imposed by deficiency of natural resources. So many gross errors have, however, been made by people obsessed with the notion that natural resources should be developed, without thinking much whether anyone wanted the products of these natural resources, that no great harm will ensue if we a little over-emphasise the other side. Already "there are some products, as for example salt, the present output of which is fully adequate for all requirements under conditions of abounding prosperity",[1] and it would be wasteful and uneconomic to insist upon exploiting further any new sources from which salt might be obtained. In varying degrees the same thing is true of many other commodities. In any event, when we reach a level of wealth where the provision of personal services becomes economically important, the importance of the limitations of physical natural resources in the narrow sense steadily diminishes. We are then much more concerned with the exploitation of human capacity (which is also perfectly "natural"), and the maintenance of a moving equilibrium in a progressive economy comes to depend more and more upon the effective organisation and education of human capacity.

Whatever doubts there may be in these circum-

[1] O. W. M. Sprague, *Recovery and Common Sense*, p. 4.

stances about the development of particular types of
employment, it is quite certain that it is neither possible nor desirable to have "an increase of production,
extending over the whole range of commodities in an
orderly and a symmetrical fashion".[1] A symmetrical
increase of production would not, as Strakosch maintains, raise the standard of life of the people, but would,
as will be argued later, lead to instability and depression. In a progressive economy, increases of production
must always be asymmetrical. In particular, it is important to note there is no ground for the belief so
widespread and influential in countries like Australia
and New Zealand, that "purely domestic industries
can expand only when the export industries expand".[2]
If the increases in wealth which material progress
brings with it encourage people to buy the products of
domestic industries and the products which indirectly
export industries make available for us here in proportions which are different from those which have
been customary in the past, there is nothing to prevent their desires from being gratified, and in that case
domestic and export industries may develop at quite
divergent rates. With things which satisfy basic or
fundamental needs, we reach the limit of satisfaction
much earlier than with other needs or desires. Many
people would find some satisfaction in buying twice as
many clothes as they at present possess, or twice as
many books, or attending twice as many concerts, seeing twice as many plays or living in houses twice the

[1] Sir Henry Strakosch, *Selected Documents submitted to the Gold
Delegation of the Financial Committee*, p. 22.

[2] Canterbury Chamber of Commerce Bulletin, No. 100. Cf. Mr
W. F. M. Ross, Country Party member in New South Wales Parliament,
July 19, 1934: "It is not possible to expand the secondary industries
unless there is a corresponding expansion of the rural industries"

size of those they at present occupy, but in the more prosperous countries, even among the poorer sections of the population, there are not many who would get much satisfaction from eating twice as much food; in general it is quite improbable that the proportionate increases in expenditure of various kinds which a higher income makes possible will be at all uniform.

The general picture which it has here been suggested we should constantly keep in mind is especially useful in offering us a guide when we are seeking an answer to two general questions which sooner or later face everybody who is interested in current controversies about the world depression. We are all familiar with complaints about over-capitalisation, excess capacity for production. Many primary industries have been over-developed. Manufacturing equipment has been wastefully duplicated, and we find great difficulty in bearing the interest burdens which have been imposed by too rapid and too costly development of certain forms of transport. All this means that much of the saving of the past has been wasted. It has been diverted into the wrong channels. But, if investors had been wiser, how would they have invested their money so as to avoid the losses which are now so obvious? For anyone who wishes to discover how far the problem of the organisation of production in a progressive economy is clearly understood by the leaders of the business community it is a useful exercise to go about putting this question to them. No satisfactory answer is possible unless we keep clearly in mind the changes in the relative importance of different kinds of demand which are certain to occur, and the fact that a satisfactory answer is so seldom given shows that the fundamental nature of these changes is seldom understood. From

quite a different point of view, the complaint is frequently made to-day that industrial recovery is checked
by selfishness, and that "a new spirit" is needed in
industry. This may well be the case, but it is not very
useful to talk about "a new spirit", unless we have
some idea of what those people who are imbued with
it are expected to do. So many of the detailed proposals put forward by people who insist upon the necessity of "a new spirit" are so diametrically opposed to
the conclusions which are suggested by our analysis
that doubts may very well be entertained as to the
value of much that is said on this subject. Anyone who
talks about the elimination of selfishness should be
asked to explain clearly what changes in the structure
of production he expects to follow from the attainment
of this admirable objective. If under the influence of
unselfish motives people do foolish things, the effects
of their foolishness are not much diminished by the
admirable quality of their motives.

Analogies drawn from one science for application to
the subject matter of another are usually misleading,
and it is now widely recognised that it is not possible
to discuss the concepts of the social sciences in narrowly mechanical terms. The interrelations between
the parts of a social structure are so complex and intimate that organic analogies seem to be much more
applicable than purely mechanical analogies. As Marshall put it (*Principles*, p. 461), "economic problems
are imperfectly presented when they are treated as
problems of statical equilibrium and not of organic
growth". But quite apart from other general objections
which have been made against regarding a society as
an organism, we find that it is impossible to discuss
the growth of a progressive economy adequately in

such terms. For this purpose the organic analogy is too
simple, and fails to bring out some of the most important cardinal points. In an ordinary organism, and
within quite a narrow range of limitations, more or less
regular ratios are maintained between the various parts
or organs. It is true that, in an ordinary organism, the
proportions between the various parts of the organism
vary at different periods of growth. The head of an infant is relatively larger than the head of an adult. But
these variations are usually confined to quite a narrow
range. If a head or a leg were to develop at much more
or much less than the normal rate of growth for the
organism as a whole, this would indicate a pathological condition which called for appropriate remedial
measures. Exactly the opposite is true of an economic
or industrial organisation. Here if any effort is made to
maintain stable relations between the various parts of
the structure, that effort by itself will create a pathological condition which will make steady growth impossible. Normal growth is out of the question unless
there is disproportionate expansion in different parts
of the structure of production.

The world has long been familiar with the virtues
of the man who made two blades of grass grow where
one grew before, and Mr Walter Elliot, the British
Minister of Agriculture, has been hailed as the man
"who made two pigs grow where one grew before".[1]
There was no doubt a time, and at no very remote
date either, when both of these activities fully merited
the highest praise that could be given them. That
time, fortunately for us, has now passed; to-day the
desire to make two pigs grow where only one grew
before is likely to degenerate into a desire to make two

[1] *Manchester Guardian*, March 9, 1934.

white elephants grow where there was only one before. We need instead statesmen and business men who will realise that in place of a single blade of grass or one pig, the world now needs a juicier blade, plus a fatter pig, plus a hat, plus a radio-set, plus a new book.

CHAPTER III

RESISTANCES TO CHANGES OF OCCUPATION AND TO CHANGES IN THE CHARACTER OF INVESTMENT

THERE are probably few people who would formally dissent from the general conclusions suggested by our analysis of the implications of material progress. Material progress must mean higher standards of living, higher average levels of real income. Higher average levels of real income mean the purchase of a much wider variety of goods and services and the satisfaction of tastes which formerly had no practical importance in determining the character of our economic organisation. Finally, the purchase of these things is impossible without a corresponding re-organisation on the side of production, and transfers of resources from the older staple industries to newer and more speculative fields.

But while there will be almost universal formal assent to these general conclusions, there is an almost equal degree of unanimity in denying the concrete propositions in which the general conclusions must inevitably be embodied. The confusion of thought which is thus revealed shows that their real meaning is in fact not at all widely understood. The widespread popular fears that technical improvements will lead to chronic and increasing unemployment are a clear illustration of this fact. Technical improvements in any one industry should make possible increased activity and increased employment in other industries. If we deny that this is possible, we deny in effect either the possibility or the desirability of material progress. Similarly, it is argued that unless foreign imports are excluded there will be no avenues for employment open for the rising generation. "What then shall we do with our boys?" If we understand the general principles enunciated above, it is clear that an adequate answer to this question is that, provided we are sensible, we shall arrange for our boys to provide the societies of which they are members with such goods and services as have in the past been inadequately supplied. Instead of this, we usually try to create a state of affairs in which our boys will be encouraged to add to the abundant supplies of things of which we already have enough.

Misunderstanding of these fundamental issues is not, however, confined to writings obviously based on popular fallacies. It also infects much of the work of expert economists. The authors of The Australian Tariff (1929), for example, revealed a similar lack of appreciation in their discussion of the alternative forms of employment which might have been developed if tariff policy had been more moderate. They were disposed to take a more favourable view of the place of the tariff in the Australian economy than would be acceptable to thoroughgoing free-traders, on the ground that, while "without the tariff it would have been possible to have obtained a larger national income per head" (p. 70), this would have been possible only on condition that population had increased more slowly. "It is not certain that if the natural course of production had been continued, it would have maintained the present population without some reduction in income per head, due to pressure upon inferior or less accessible land or to lower prices for a greater volume of exports" (p. 32). It was rightly affirmed that "in any alternative to a protective policy, new production must be found to take the place of the production absolutely dependent on the tariff" (p. 71), but throughout it was implicitly assumed that the only important type of new production which could be developed to replace relatively inefficient protected manufactures was primary production, designed to expand export trade. The wide range of "tertiary" products whose importance might be expected to grow if a relaxation of tariff restrictions made possible a higher average level of productivity was practically ignored.

Mr Lloyd George's broadcast in the "Whither Britain?" series illustrates the same tendency. For a solution of the problem of chronic unemployment, which would provide permanent employment for the whole population, "the most hopeful method that has always occurred to me has been the better utilisation of the resources of our soil. Only 6·8 per cent of our population are employed on the land. If we had the same percentage of people on the soil as the next lowest country, we should in a few years have absorbed all the chronic unemployment and this minimum of a million would have been employed in the healthiest of all occupations." [1]

Mr Walter Elliot, the British Minister of Agriculture, expressed a similar point of view in a more picturesque phrase when he warned the Dominions that "when you lock us out of the factories, you lock us into the fields". To Mr Elliot the existence of unused capacity suggests

[1] *Manchester Guardian*, March 21, 1934.

not the provision of more of the numerous things which are still in short supply, but instead a further fillip to the production of things which are already over-abundant.

(i) *Agriculture*

Indeed the illustration which is most important for practical policy of refusal to admit the implications of material progress is to be found in the view which is practically world-wide of the proper place of agriculture in any national economy. Nearly everywhere there is a stubborn prejudice in favour of maintaining the number of agriculturists at least at the level customary in the past, even although the increased command over the forces of nature which science now enables us to exercise makes it much easier than ever before to provide adequate supplies for everybody of the products of agriculture. In every country there is an energetic opposition to anything which seems likely to diminish the relative importance of agriculture as a field of employment, and agricultural policy is deliberately aimed at the maintenance or the increase of output, of area under cultivation and of the number of persons employed.

It appears to be widely believed that there is some natural ratio which ought to be preserved, apparently without reference to the volume of output, between the number of people engaged in so-called primary production and the numbers engaged in other kinds of work. No attempt has ever been made to define precisely the correct ratio, but it has been generally agreed that the tendency which has been observed almost everywhere for urban population to increase more rapidly than population in rural districts, the so-called "Drift to the

Towns", is something certainly to be deplored, and if possible reversed, or at least held in check. Politicians who differ about everything else have been practically unanimous about the dangers of the drift to the towns. In "new" countries, like Australia and New Zealand, it has been generally assumed that immigration should be encouraged mainly for the development of agricultural and pastoral production, for the products of which it has been quite erroneously and uncritically assumed that the "market is practically unlimited".[1]

This population trend has been observed in so many countries with the widest variety of economic structure that it is difficult to believe that it can anywhere be adequately explained by reference to purely local conditions or local policy. Clearly the only satisfactory test for determining the optimum number of farmers in any country or in the world as a whole is their ability to supply the food and raw materials which the community needs. If anything happens to increase the efficiency of their production, the optimum number of farmers will diminish. After a certain rather low standard of income has been passed, the demand for food is not greatly stimulated by any fall in price which increased efficiency makes possible. People prefer rather to spend the money they save through getting food more cheaply on other things, on clothes, housing and other needs, familiar and unfamiliar, because happily, as Adam Smith pointed out long ago, the capacity of the human stomach is limited. There can be little doubt that improvements in agriculture have in fact made these changes in expenditure possible. The resources of science, advances in chemistry, botany, biology, bacteriology, have, during recent years, been directed on a quite

[1] Canterbury Chamber of Commerce Bulletin, May 1929.

unprecedented scale towards the improvement of farm methods throughout the world; there have been marked changes in the use of fertilisers, improvements in the quality of live stock, in seed selection and in scientific soil study, as well as in the application to farming of machinery and other improved implements. An accurate quantitative statement is difficult, or perhaps impossible, but the guess may safely be hazarded that during this generation the significance of new inventions affecting agriculture has been greater than the significance of any other set of new inventions. The inevitable consequence is that the world can now get all the food it needs with a relatively diminished expenditure of human effort, and some of the resources thus set free can be applied with advantage to the production of other things. In a very poor community which has not previously been properly fed, the fall of price which improved food production makes possible will stimulate a greater demand, more food will be produced, and at least the same number of people will continue to be employed in food production. But if the community is already well fed, it will not want all the extra food which any technical improvement makes it possible to produce; some of those originally employed in food production will find themselves unemployed unless they are transferred to other kinds of work.

What is to become of them? Speaking in terms of purchasing power, the improvements would show their effects to the individual income-receiver in lower prices, or if the price-fall is checked, in higher profits for some of the producers; if they do not wish to buy more food than in the past, they will find that they have more money to spend on other things. The problem of readjustment under these circumstances is the problem of getting the surplus men into the industries which will produce the other things. If the improvements are sufficiently radical and widespread, some people will want to experiment with the enjoyment of entirely new things and, to re-establish equilibrium, new industries must then be opened up.

The greatest difficulty has, however, been experienced in getting the conclusions from this reasoning translated in terms of public policy. Nobody would regard it as a matter for satisfaction if it were discovered that the railways were employing more men than were necessary to give us an adequate transport service, or that there were more doctors than were necessary to keep us healthy. It would be generally agreed that this would be wasteful, and that it would be better for the surplus engine-drivers and medical men to get on with useful work of some other kind. But if a similar situation is found to exist in a farming industry, little eagerness is displayed to draw the same sensible and inevitable conclusion. All sorts of sophisms are used to show that the industry is really not over-crowded, and all sorts of plans devised to avoid the necessity for anyone being "driven off the land".

At a time when it is less necessary than ever before in the world's history to extend the area devoted to food production, each country makes strenuous efforts to become as self-sufficient as possible in this field, and as the exporting countries refuse to relax their efforts, there is an inevitable glut and a catastrophic fall of prices. Price movements are resisted by means of pools and export controls designed to facilitate the dumping of surplus production abroad, the ultimate effect being still further to stimulate production which cannot be profitably disposed of with further price-declines and further dislocation of the whole economic machine.

The belief that a relative decline in agricultural population is undesirable is not confined to politicians and journalists who might be excused for failing to make an exhaustive analysis of the production machinery of a progressive economy. It has also been supported by eminent academic authorities whose business it is to make such analyses. "It is the country districts in the Dominions", said Carr-Saunders,[1] "which require developing; the proportion of urban population to rural population is already excessive." "In certain fundamental respects", said the Report of the British Liberal Industrial Inquiry, "the remedy for the present unsatisfactory position of British agriculture is the same as that suggested in the case of our great export industries—the taking of such steps as will secure an increased net return per head of those engaged. The resulting increased product per acre and per head will make possible a proportionately increased return to those engaged, whilst at the same time leading to an increase in the area under cultivation and to an increase in the numbers engaged."[2] Similarly in 1926 an American economist declared that "it is easy to conceive of a different working of our so-called competitive system that would give us more farmers and better rewards at the same time",[3] but in neither case was the method for achieving these allegedly desirable, but apparently inconsistent, objectives defined with any precision.

Not only was the trend of population movement

---

[1] *Population*, p. 88.   [2] Pp. 326-7.
[3] John D. Black, *American Economic Review*, Supplement, March 1926, p. 138.

which was the inevitable consequence of material progress widely condemned before the depression, and strenuous efforts made to keep it in check, but during the depression also the view has been held in the most widely assorted quarters that one—some would say, the most important—way to diminish unemployment was through the further extension of farming industries. It might be imagined that the most sensible plan would be to look about for industries that are doing comparatively well, and to encourage their expansion. Instead of this, there is a high degree of unanimity in favour of the view that the proper thing to do is to extend those industries which are already the most depressed. People complain bitterly about the hard lot and the small income of the farmer, but at the same time demand that a larger number of people should be induced or compelled to submit themselves to the same miserable fate. In face of the obvious fact that farming is relatively unprofitable to-day, the view has recently been expressed (by the Secretary of the Auckland Boys' Employment Committee) that "what is required is a change in psychology which would encourage young men to regard farming as a profitable vocation". More curious still, the farmer himself is ready to give vigorous support to policies of this kind. A lawyer or a doctor who is finding difficulty in making what he regards as an adequate income does not as a rule urge the Government to take steps to induce more people to become lawyers or doctors. He is much more likely to go about telling people that the professions are grossly overcrowded, and that by raising entrance standards and by other restrictive measures the number of new entrants should be diminished. He may even urge upon the

young men about him the duty of getting back to the
land, and it is surprising that he should so often suc-
ceed in convincing farmers too of the justice of his
arguments. The farmer's desire to get more people
on the land is no doubt often merely an expression of
his desire to have abundant supplies of cheap labour
at his disposal, but it also goes much further than this,
revealing a profound misconception of the reasons
which in fact make land settlement desirable.

In face of the serious marketing troubles which beset
most primary industries to-day, it is becoming increasingly difficult to maintain that the extension
of land settlement is at the moment more than a palliative, deserving support because the only apparent
alternative is to maintain large numbers of men from
relief funds. "At least", it is said, "a man on the land
can feed himself." As one Australian supporter of large-
scale migration put it, "I hope no one will exclaim, 'But
where are you going to dispose of the produce of this
new settlement?' Even if a million new-comers succeeded only in feeding themselves, Australia would be
that much stronger for their presence." [1] This belief is
nevertheless sometimes pushed so far as to become the
basis of a long-term policy. It is suggested that groups
of unemployed who have been induced to settle on the
land should organise themselves in small independent
communities cut off as far as possible from contacts
with wider markets. A recent statement by Sir John
Russell, who is probably better acquainted than anyone else with the technical side of agricultural improvements, illustrates this point of view: "My feeling", he
said, "is that we should do well to work out possibilities
of a system of colonies producing not for the world

[1] *Sydney Morning Herald*, February 8, 1934.

market but simply for themselves. These colonies would simply set out to live, arranging as much leisure as they could. They would be free from the risk of the struggle for place in the world market." From the standpoint of taking advantage of the opportunities for civilised life which scientific advance offers to us, this attitude is pure defeatism. The intellectual effort involved in working out the details of the necessary adaptations is apparently thought to be too severe; therefore, it is suggested, we must abandon the struggle. There is no doubt something to be said for the view that economic advancement is an illusion, but if we adopt this view, we should at least be clear in our minds as to what we are doing; we should understand that we are deliberately refusing to other people any opportunity of achieving the same economic standards as are thought to be reasonable for the community as a whole.[1]

It has been commonly supposed that our supplies of land should be utilised in such a way as will make possible the maximum volume of employment upon the land. But this is quite erroneous. Provided we are already getting as much as we need of the direct products of land cultivation, there is no reason for being concerned if we discover that some areas are not being used to their fullest capacity. The only ultimately satisfactory foundation for employment is the provision of goods and services which other people will want to buy. If it happens that this involves more cultivation of the land, the agricultural population will tend to keep up. If it involves work which is not directly connected with the land, the relative importance of agricultural popu-

---

[1] For a more detailed discussion of the whole of this question, see "The Drift to the Towns", *Economic Record*, November 1929; cf. also "The Rural Exodus in Germany", International Labour Office Studies and Reports, Series K, No. 12, especially chs. i. and iv.

lation will decline, and there are no valid reasons why we should become alarmed about it.

It is quite a mistake to suppose that because things are "essential" it is impossible to over-produce them. The production of essential things should no doubt be our first concern, but when adequate supplies are available it is foolish and wasteful to insist upon producing more. The standards by reference to which we will determine to what extent a thing is essential must depend upon varying conditions. According to Mrs. Barbara Wootton, in Russia at one time "the production of pencils for Government offices was scheduled as a shock industry of special importance. The step was not wholly unreasonable, since, in circumstances in which the whole feeding of a people depends on Government decree, the provision of pencils with which Government officials can record their observations and decisions may fairly claim to be a prior condition of any economic activity whatever."[1] But even when pencil production was regarded as absolutely essential, nobody imagined that it was impossible to over-develop it. A similar truth should be equally obvious in relation to food production. Moreover, if food production becomes more efficient, a decline in agricultural population is quite consistent with an increase in agricultural output. It is the supply of food which is important, not the number of people employed in producing it.

It is not claimed that this is a complete account of all the deeply rooted sentiments and prejudices which give to the development of agriculture such a widespread popular appeal,[2] and make the world as a whole want more farmers than it needs. Agricultural work

[1] *Plan or No Plan*, p. 59.
[2] Attempts have even been made to offer a Freudian explanation.

has often been supposed to have a special social value, and especially during the last few years the trend towards the over-development of agriculture has been largely an expression of nationalist sentiment, based upon the fear of War. Whatever the influences may be which have made this trend so powerful, however, the action to which they lead is exactly contrary to that which a reasonable progressive economy would demand.

(ii) *Manufactures and Tariffs*

Important as agriculture is in this connection, it is, however, only one illustration of a much more general trend. The common view of the value of protective tariffs is based upon precisely the same foundations. One of the trump cards usually played by tariff advocates is the fear of unemployment, which means in effect a denial of the possibility of developing any types of production other than those which are already in existence. But if manufacturing technique in any industry increases so much in efficiency that all reasonable demands can be met by using less than the aggregate capital equipment which happens to be in existence at the time, any attempt by protective measures or otherwise to keep the whole equipment going, much more any attempt to expand it, must lead to glut and over-production. It is not the least of the evils of economic nationalism that it leads, through the medium of tariff protection, to over-development of productive capacity in many important manufacturing industries. The belief that a tariff will reduce the volume of unemployment is dangerous because it encourages the notion that we need further expansion of the industries which are already well

developed. It means taking too static a view of the
problem of labour distribution. We find that people
are unemployed in the iron and steel or the woollen
industries; the tariff argument suggests that we should
endeavour to get them back into the same industries,
whereas in a progressive economy the only solution
which is thoroughly satisfactory is one which will
divert part of the superfluous streams of labour into
new channels of employment.

In recent years the advances of science in manufacturing industry have on a superficial view perhaps
not appeared so dramatic as the advances of the last
century. Their importance has, however, been very
great, and though the limit of consumers' demand at
profitable prices is not as a rule so quickly reached as
in agriculture, it *is* eventually reached sooner or later,
and it becomes desirable to transfer to new fields some
of the labour and capital which scientific advance has
rendered superfluous in the old. If improved methods
of production make motor-cars cheaper, the demand
for motor-cars is likely for a time to extend so that at
least as many people as before can be employed in
this industry, but eventually even here demand will
be satiated, and transfers will be necessary. The inevitable effect of the maintenance, and still more of
the raising of tariff barriers, is to delay these necessary
transfers.

The refusal to admit the necessity for change which
is involved in the erection of tariff barriers finds its
most emphatic expression at the present time in the
controversy about Japanese competition. Depreciated
currency and other factors are no doubt important,
but stripped of all the complications and irrelevances
which have crept into the discussion, the problem is

substantially this. By various means the Japanese have increased the efficiency of their production in certain lines in such a way as to threaten well-established producers in other countries. The low level of Japanese wages naturally attracts attention in discussions of this point, but it is probably true that while Japanese wages are lower than those common in more advanced Western countries, their level is substantially higher than that which prevailed in Japan twenty years ago. In other words, as one might have expected, the improvements in efficiency which have made Japanese competition in foreign markets more keen have also made possible a higher standard of wages inside Japan. The average Japanese factory-worker probably receives a higher income than he would if he remained at work in agriculture. In the case of a small self-contained group, any marked improvement in the efficiency of one or two members of the group would reasonably be interpreted as a signal to the others that they should not waste their time doing the same sort of work as more efficient individuals were successfully attempting. The extension from a small self-contained group to large interconnected national groups does not introduce any fundamentally new factor, although the complexity of the organisation certainly makes the change-over in the character of work demanded from some individuals much more difficult. In a rational world which understood the extent to which Japanese competition was the result of increased efficiency, other groups elsewhere would be happy to enjoy the benefits arising from the performance of work which formerly had been to a large extent neglected, but to which could now be devoted the resources no longer needed for producing goods with which the Japanese are successfully competing. The fact that changes such as these are likely to be enormously difficult does not alter the fact that the changes themselves are sensible and in some degree inevitable. This is, however, far from the common attitude to Japanese competition. Persons already engaged in industries threatened with Japanese competition feel that there is a clear case for excluding Japanese goods from their markets. Sometimes this point of view is expressed as an objection to low wage standards in Japan. That the real problem is not one of low wage standards but of threatened displacement of labour and capital is shown clearly by the fact that protectionists are not as a rule any more willing to admit competition from countries where wage standards are high. But apart from this point, there is an obvious dilemma in pressing the charge of low wage standards against Japan. In effect the Japanese are told that if they raise their wage-levels there will be no objection to their competition, but if the volume of Japanese goods in certain industries makes it necessary in a free market for some other producers to change their work, this necessity will not in any way be diminished by the payment of higher Japanese wages. The claim indeed that Japanese wages should be raised is little more than an expression of the hope that if the wage-levels were improved the Japanese would find it impossible to produce in competition with the older units, a conclusion obviously not very beneficial to the Japanese.

It is even more curious that the significance of this point is little appreciated by many of those who profess themselves to be quite sympathetic to Japanese industrial development. The industrialisation of Japan is presented quite fairly as the only method whereby Japan can satisfactorily maintain her large population. Many non-Japanese have recognised in general terms the force of the Japanese claims to be allowed to encourage industrial growth. This sympathy, however, is often expressed only in the vague form which suggests conference in the hope that something will turn up. Actually if Japanese industrialisation is encouraged and if the Japanese are allowed to seek such markets elsewhere as they might reasonably claim, it is quite inevitable that one consequence of their industrial growth will be a relative decline in the importance in certain other countries of industries already established there. It merely clouds the issue and encourages woolliness of thought, if it is supposed that the Japanese case can be met without the necessity for any such changes.

The whole problem of the exploration of new markets which to-day seems to many people so bewildering cannot indeed be properly understood except in the light of the implications of material progress. The course of industrial expansion in the nineteenth century has frequently been described in terms of the exploitation of new markets, opened up by the establishment of trade connections with hitherto undeveloped countries, and made easier by the rapid world-wide growth of population. Now that the rate of population growth is slackening, and many of the backward countries are developing their own manufacturing industries, it is argued by many people that the day of expanding markets is over. The difficulties which people experience in visualising the character of the new markets which are likely to develop in the future arise in effect from their refusal to think in terms of anything but the goods which are already being produced. Even when manufacturers are concerned not merely with conserving positions which they already occupy, but also with extending their activities, it is rare for them to look much further than the prospect of winning for themselves part of the market which is already occupied by others. Often they do not even seriously claim that they will be able to turn out goods better than those which are already being produced. They admit instead that they will probably produce them a little worse, but insist that that does not seriously damage their claim for reservation of some part of the existing market. The possibility of making genuine additions to the aggregate volume of production does not greatly interest them; they are anxious merely to drive out some existing form of production, and substitute for it another, a procedure which is clearly unlikely to confer any substantial benefit upon the community as a whole. It is the prevalence of this point of view which explains the chronic tendency towards over-development of productive capacity which manufacturing industries so frequently display. It is part of the normal stock-in-trade of manufacturers' tariff propaganda to maintain that, if all the local equipment in existence were used to its fullest capacity, a much larger part of the local market could be adequately met by local producers. This is equivalent to boasting that the stream of savings has in the past been misdirected, and that the capital equipment in these industries has been expanded beyond reasonable limits. It is natural that individuals who have made errors should seek protection against the consequences of their folly; it is unreasonable that the community should be asked to congratulate itself upon the muddle which has thus been created.

Even if we are prepared to go a little further than a reshuffling of existing markets, and seriously consider the possibility of expanding production and not merely of driving other competitors out, there is an equally strong tendency to think that the limits of such expansion will be determinately fixed by the low purchasing power of the inhabitants of countries to whom the increased supplies of goods might be offered. The belief that this low purchasing power is a factor which is incapable of variation is itself nothing but a further expression of the deep-rooted mental habit of thinking in terms of a static, instead of a progressive, economy. It is true that markets in the East, for example, are limited because the purchasing power of the Chinese, the Indian, the Japanese, the Javanese, is low. The purchasing power of these people is low, however, only because their production is low. Ultimately the only way of increasing their purchasing power is to increase their production. If, however, their production is increased, it is probable that at least a large part of it will be along lines which will compete with other producers elsewhere, and to this the only response which is rational in the long run is a further transfer of resources into other undeveloped or entirely new fields.

The natural consequence of the manufacturer's point of view which is here being criticised is excessive productive capacity. Its effects, however, appear in manufacturing industries in rather a different form from that which they take in agriculture. In agriculture the individual often finds it difficult, or thinks it inadvisable, to reduce his output when prices fall below a profitable level. He is often indeed advised to maintain output at all costs. The manufacturer, however, can more readily adjust his production programme when his prices fall, and excessive production capacity therefore tends to show itself less in a visible glut of commodities than in idle equipment and unemployment.

(iii) *Professional Work and "Tertiary" Product*

The third wide field in which resistance to change upsets the smooth working of our economic organisation can best be approached by observing the attitude commonly adopted towards the admission of increasing numbers of people to the newer types of work which must inevitably develop as wealth increases. If the essential transfers of resources are to be carried through smoothly and effectively, not only must people not be discouraged from leaving the old fields of activity, but barriers must not be raised to prevent their entering the new. The attitude which is important here expresses itself in two quite different ways. Sometimes there is a feeling almost of contempt for educational and social services and similar "tertiary" activities which tend to be regarded as parasitic, instead of being, as they must be, the inevitable fruit of the processes of increasing wealth.[1] We are still too much under the influence of Adam Smith's unfortunate phrase, "unproductive labour", and tell each other that we cannot live on luxuries. Curiously enough, the only service of this kind which appeals to many people is the one example, military and naval service, which may quite confidently be condemned as wasteful, and which inevitably leads to a lowering of the average income-level.

[1] Cf. Stuart Chase, *Economy of Abundance*, p. 218. "The service trades, however useful—and most of them are not useful at all—are parasitic on the physical output of the plant. It must feed, clothe, shelter and energize them. They are a kind of debt against it—and there is a limit to the burdensome possibilities of all debt."

This feeling sometimes shows itself in the most un-expected quarters. Emil Lederer, for example, in dis-cussing technological unemployment, says that under certain circumstances "the only possible outlet is in the direction of personal services, the absorptive capacity of which is fairly high when the rates of remuneration for them are rapidly falling,"[1] but the tone of his discussion suggests that this is not really a way out or at least that the provision of employ-ment through personal services is merely a second-best solution. The truth, however, is exactly the opposite of this; ultimately the only satisfactory solution of problems of technological unemployment lies in the more rapid expansion of personal services and other types of work akin to personal services.

In practice more important than this feeling of con-tempt is the fact that barriers are maintained or raised to limit entry into the professions and similar "tertiary" types of work. In a poor community few people can be spared for work of these kinds. In a wealthy community it is inevitable and desirable that the number of workers in these departments should increase, but fearful lest the quasi-monopolistic privi-leges which they have been in the habit of enjoying should be destroyed, those who are already at work there raise the cry that "the professions are over-crowded". The new industries which it is desirable to expand are on the whole likely to be those which are relatively more prosperous, so that the position can be described by saying that if equilibrium is to be pre-served, people must not be unduly hampered in attempting to enter the occupations which are best paid. This, however, is exactly what is always happen-

---

[1] *International Labour Review*, July 1933, p. 18.

ing. Barriers of various kinds, costs of training, professional restrictions, social prejudices,[1] are all effective in restricting the supply of people for the more highly paid work. These checks help to create the glut in other parts of the field of production and this not merely keeps income-levels down in the overcrowded areas, but also sets up reactions which cause more unemployment elsewhere. If conditions exist which make possible a higher average income-level, the realisation of these possibilities may at the same time necessitate an absolute and almost certainly a relative decline in the incomes paid to certain groups in the community. Their efforts to check this decline may not only keep the average level down, but also in the long run cause embarrassment to many members of these favoured groups.

A full analysis of the widespread effects of professional exclusiveness would indeed carry us very far into the heart of the most radical antinomies of our social organisation. If material progress demands a more rapid inflow of entrants into the more highly paid types of work, and if those who are already engaged there, reluctant to permit of any relaxation of

---

[1] It is seldom that social prejudice is so frankly and naïvely expressed as by Sir R. Burton Chadwick, M.P., in discussing the type of boy who should be encouraged to qualify as an officer in the merchant navy (cit. *Manchester Guardian*, July 29, 1931). The point of view which he disclosed nevertheless still has great influence even in allegedly democratic countries. "Here", he said, "is a calling which involves the leadership of men and the giving of the word of command. These very high responsibilities demand character, brain, courage, and generally, the principles that govern the life of a gentleman. All the forces of government, charity, and political life are directed and quite rightly directed to helping the boys of what is described as the working class. None of this effort, generally speaking, is directed to the boy of the professional class. He has to look after himself. There in the officer rank in the merchant navy is a calling which might well and fairly be conserved for this class of boy."

their privileges, take steps to check this inflow their resistance will gravely endanger the stability of the whole economic structure.

The provision of the new types of service which material progress demands will be difficult or impossible unless there is a parallel improvement in general standards of education. If a rapidly progressing society needs large additions to the ranks of musicians, medical men and other purveyors of personal services, our educational policy must be moulded to make possible a larger supply of these people. But as general standards of education rise, the scarcity value of the services sold by educated persons will tend to diminish, and the opportunities for earning incomes much above the average by the performance of professional work will accordingly be restricted. This consequence is likely to be distasteful to the people whose incomes are above the average, and they tend to be critical of extensions of education which may threaten their privileged position.

While the effects of better education upon the production of wealth have been widely emphasised and realised, much less attention has, for various reasons, been given to its equally important effects upon income distribution. There is, however, good reason for supposing that improved standards of education are an important, if incomplete, explanation of the world-wide trend, which has been so much discussed since the War, towards a narrower margin between skilled and unskilled wage rates. The most important reason why the wages of unskilled workers have been relatively so low is that there are always far too many of them, and the steady extension of primary and to a less extent, of secondary education, which has been such an important fact in the social and political evolution of recent years, is precisely a method which might have been expected to increase relatively the number of people who had skilled labour to offer for sale. Anything which increased their number would at the same time diminish the comparative value of the skilled work which they performed, and this is exactly what has happened.[1] A similar tendency is likely to affect professional incomes no less than the wages of skilled artisans. If the natural trend is resisted, or barriers are raised to check the entry of new competitors, the effects upon the stability of the economic structure as a whole will be similar to the effects of other monopolistic price-controls, or of any chronic tendency to over-supply staple industries with capital.

There is indeed a threefold connection between educational policy and material progress. First, improved standards of education may themselves be an independent force initiating the course of material progress, and therefore making necessary the adjustments which we have been discussing. Secondly, whatever the original cause of the change, educational services are likely to be included among the things which a progressive society is likely to demand in increasing quantities. And thirdly, whether there is a direct demand or not for more education, more extensive facilities will be necessary if there is to be an adequate supply of people competent to perform the other newer skilled services which a progressive society is likely to demand. The third point may be alternatively expressed by saying that in the distribution of savings it is as important to make an adequate allocation for the cultivation of

[1] "Education and Income Distribution", *International Labour Review*, June 1932; cf. Dalton, *Inequality of Income*, p. 264-7.

human resources of various kinds for the performance of work of the "tertiary" type as it is to have
supplies of material capital available in the correct
proportions.

The problem of determining appropriate standards
for entry into skilled or professional work is undoubtedly complex, and criticism in particular cases may
often be unfair. It can scarcely be denied, however,
that reasonable methods for maintaining entrance
qualifications pass very easily in practice into unreasonable methods for restricting entry, and thus creating
artificial scarcity of various kinds of labour. This transition is as likely to be made in the imposition of standards for entry into the professions as in the maintenance of apprenticeship regulations by trade unions,
which have often been so much criticised.

The most complete study of professional organisations in Great Britain is by A. M. Carr-Saunders and
P. A. Wilson.[1] These writers are by no means unsym-
pathetic to the point of view of professional men and
conclude that there is no substance in complaints that
examination standards are too high.[2] Nevertheless they
agree "that the cost of entering certain professions is
higher than it need be in the interests of efficiency and
that the professional associations are not free from
blame for the position".[3] The complaints which have
been common nearly everywhere in recent years about
overcrowding in the professions, and in particular the
lively interest taken by professional associations during the depression in proposals for limiting the number
of new entrants have made it increasingly difficult to
believe that these associations are concerned merely

---

[1] *The Professions.* Oxford University Press, 1933.
[2] P. 374.   [3] P. 386.

with the maintenance of a high standard of professional qualifications. In some instances, in Germany and Denmark, and no doubt in other countries as well, the complainants have quite openly and honestly argued that the only adequate remedy for their grievances is a check on the supply of new professional workers.[1] It is natural that people should like to conceal even from themselves the cruder foundations of such restrictive policy, but it cannot be doubted that in England, for example, the attempts to limit the entry of women into the medical profession are based in part upon the desire to protect the customary level of income for medical men. In New Zealand a member of the legal profession brought before the Council of the Victoria University College, Wellington, a resolution (which the Council did not accept) that "it is undesirable at the present time that students should be encouraged to pursue the study of law for vocational purposes".[2] Similarly in Australia, the editor of *The General Practitioner*, believing that "all over the world the ratio of doctors to patients was not only too high nearly everywhere, but also was gradually increasing",[3] urged "the limitation of the number of entrants into the profession by raising the preliminary examination hurdles". "The result would be fewer doctors, earning a better livelihood, which would be to the benefit of the public as well as the profession."[4] At the same time steps have been taken in New Zealand to limit the enrolment at the University of students proposing to take the medical

---

[1] Prinzing, "Die statistische Beurteilung des Bedarfs an Aerzten und damit der Aussichten für den Nachwuchs", *Deutsche Medizinische Wochenschrift*, August 15, 1930. "As a protection against the proletarisation of the medical profession, the only means which remains is to make admission to the medical course difficult."

[2] April 29, 1932.   [3] May 15, 1933.   [4] March 15, 1933.

course. The alarm which has been widely expressed at the possibility of an influx of German medical men illustrates clearly the same point. It would be unfair to suggest that little or no attention was paid to the provision of that volume of professional service which the community needs, but it cannot be denied that in estimating the volume it is regarded as a *sine qua non* that the customary level of professional income should not be lowered. As a British writer quoted in *The General Practitioner* put it,[1] if the over-supply of doctors is not checked, "the medical organisations are likely to find themselves powerless to exercise any control over methods of practice, over professional ethics, or standards of remuneration".[2] Wage-earners are sometimes reproached as being short-sighted and irrational in attaching excessive importance to the maintenance of customary standards of living, but undue respect for customary standards is just as common among other classes of the community with higher average income-levels.

Actually in a rapidly progressive society, considerable increases in the relative numerical importance of certain groups of professional workers might be quite consistent with the maintenance of their customary

[1] June 15, 1933.

[2] Cf. Dr. A. Gregory, in moving a resolution urging the desirability of raising the age of registration of medical students to eighteen years, at the 102nd Annual Meeting of the British Medical Association at Bournemouth: "The profession had reached saturation point and the time had come to take action to limit the number of those who sought to join the ranks of the profession. While there was probably room for a better distribution of practitioners and perhaps for a larger number of doctors, the economic factor was at the moment of paramount consideration. The bulk of the profession had suffered a diminution of their income, and there was a grave danger of the social and ethical standards being greatly lowered and the best traditions of the profession impaired" (*Manchester Guardian*, July 21, 1934).

absolute level of income. The general increase of wealth would mean a relatively rapid increase of demand for their services, the value of which would therefore tend to rise if the supply were not allowed to expand at much the same rate.

The general validity of the argument which has here been elaborated in favour of a relatively slow development of primary, and a relatively rapid development of "tertiary" industries is sometimes admitted, but the admission is combined with insistence that its practical implications for the country where the speaker happens to live are nevertheless to be rejected. It is agreed that it is generally desirable that certain agricultural industries or certain manufacturing activities which have been over-developed should be contracted, but all the inconveniences of contraction, and of seeking for alternative fields of production, it is argued, should be borne by people in other countries. This view has been widely held in Australia and New Zealand. According to the Auckland Chamber of Commerce *Journal*, for example,[1] the thesis that the urban drift of population is in harmony with the requirements of material progress, "stated as a world-wide principle is probably more or less sound; but as applied to New Zealand, the urban drift may be a serious disaster if this country is ill-adapted for the production of comforts and luxuries. . . In view of the present world-wide tendency in farm production, it behoves us in New Zealand to bend every effort to increasing the percentage of the world demand for our farm products that New Zealand can supply. . . . The urban drift may quite well be the symptom of a tendency which is a blessing for the world generally, and

---

[1] May 1, 1929, p. 12.

yet prove a disaster for New Zealand." If views like
this are at all widespread, the adaptations which are
desirable will be indefinitely delayed with inevitable
general dislocation as the consequence. The whole
machinery of negotiating trade treaties is profoundly
affected by this point of view. Everybody waits for
someone else to begin, and in the end little or nothing
is done. The difficulties created in Australia and New
Zealand in 1934 by the threat of quota restrictions are
an adequate commentary on the view expressed in
1929, that these countries should "bend every effort
to increasing the percentage of the world demand for
farm products", which they could supply.

(iv) *Depressed Industries—a Metaphorical Confusion*

Reluctance to follow through to the end the consequences of this reasoning is in part no doubt due to
mere stupidity, but stupidity is reinforced by the
influence of a mischievous metaphor which has an
irresistible lure for many thinkers and writers who deal
with the difficulties of depressed industries.

The graceful use of metaphor is doubtless an effective
weapon in any literary armoury, and even the dullest
and most prosaic of economists cannot completely
steel himself against its attractions. But if taken for
more than they are really worth, metaphors are likely
to distort or deceive. Every economist is familiar with
the sad results, so devastating to clear thinking, of the
common habit of talking of trade in terms appropriate
only to military conflict; there is, however, another
metaphor the misuse of which is no less damaging to
sound industrial policy, but which, because it is much

more subtle, has attracted less attention.

In times of depression we naturally think a good deal about methods for reviving trade, and our inveterate habit of speaking metaphorically as if industries were individuals with personalities and lives of their own usually leads us to take it for granted that it is those industries which are most depressed which most need encouragement. It is a natural healthy human instinct to stand up for individuals who have fallen on evil days; what then could be more obvious and proper than that we should apply the same admirable humanitarian practice to industries? Paradoxical as at first sight it may sound, it can, however, be made abundantly clear that the sensible policy to pursue at all times, whether in depression or not, is to encourage the further development, not of industries which are depressed, but of industries which are prosperous.

It is quite right, both economically and humanly, to assist individuals who are weak or dispirited, but obviously the aid which will be most effective and which has the best chance of bringing permanent results will not be something which encourages the unfortunate individual to struggle for a place in an industry where everybody is already depressed, but rather something which makes it easy for him to get into an industry which is relatively prosperous. Even at the worst of times, such industries are to be found. Naturally we hear much less about them, because the people engaged in them have no serious grievances, and seldom advertise their prosperity. And yet, curiously enough, though the shrewd business man would not think for a moment of advising his friends, and, in particular, his son, if they happened to be looking about for business openings, to select those where the chances of success were obviously poor, the very same man will often earnestly beseech the Government to take steps to expand depressed industries. These steps can be effective only if other men can be persuaded to do exactly the opposite of what he would insist to be wise for his own friends or his own family.

This unfortunate metaphorical confusion is in part responsible for our mistaken attitude towards the respective claims of flourishing and depressed industries. Everybody wants to be more prosperous, but nobody wants to leave the occupation in which fortune, good or bad, has placed him. We talk a great deal about over-production, and the old rather formal and academic argument of economic theorists that general over-production is impossible is distinctly out of fashion. It is indeed quite probable that the world has produced too much wheat, and perhaps too much rubber and coffee and sugar and other things, but instead of frankly facing the obvious consequences of this and turning our attention to the production of things of which we have not yet by any means got too much, we spend much useless time and energy in working out arrangements which will make it possible for everybody who is already engaged in these over-productive industries to remain comfortably there instead of insisting that some of them must get out and produce something else. Farming will not become a profitable vocation in consequence of any "change in psychology". It will become profitable only when we correct the ratio, which is at present too high, of the number engaged in farming to the number employed in other occupations.

The unintelligent desire to avoid the necessity for changes in the character of work and investment could also be easily illustrated in many other directions. The widespread prejudice against the employment of women, which in some countries has recently been elevated to the status of a major point in State policy, rests at bottom on little more than this. If women can perform certain services more cheaply or more effectively than the men who have become accustomed to doing such work, there is no valid reason for refusing to allow them to do so, provided the appropriate steps are taken to discover new outlets for the labour resources which are then released for other work. Insistence that men shall be protected from the risks of change of this kind is no more defensible than is any other of the forms which objections to the implications of material progress have taken. It is clearly absurd to suppose that material progress should be encouraged, and at the same time to insist that large numbers of intelligent and educated persons should be prevented from making any contribution to the national income. The sex of the intelligent persons is quite irrelevant. No one could doubt that, if we kept in idleness say one-third of the male population which is normally employed, the income-level of the community as a whole would be lower than it need be. Exactly the same conclusion must be accepted if we refuse to allow women to work.

(v) *The Price and Profit Mechanism*

It has already been pointed out that while on account of the magnitude of the scale on which material progress to-day demands transfers of labour and capital, these transfers are likely to present problems which in practice may be regarded as new, they are essentially very old problems and have already frequently found adequate solutions. Before, therefore, we consider the conditions which are likely to determine the magnitude of the adjustments which are now necessary, or which are likely to stimulate resistance to change, we should recall briefly how, in fact, the adjustments have been made in the past.

An answer to this question demands an analysis of the mechanism of price-change and the function of profit in modern industry. The initiative in industrial change must rest for the most part with the entrepreneur, the active business man. The individual workman in a complicated society where the division of labour is developed to a high degree cannot easily find alternative employment without the co-operation of the people who control capital. This is not a peculiarity of capitalist society. It is equally true in Russia and would be true in any co-operative organisation. Consider first a hypothetical isolated case, the introduction of more efficient methods into an industry working under competitive conditions and producing goods for which the demand is inelastic. Competition will compel producers to lower prices a little and demand may be slightly extended, but if there is no adjustment of the supplies of labour and capital employed in the industry, demand will not extend far enough to keep up the previous level of net returns and the rate of profit on the capital invested will therefore tend to fall. This should indicate to producers the unwisdom of further increasing investment in that industry, and there will at the same time be less employment there. Sometimes it is necessary to reduce wages as an indication of the unwisdom of training for that particular type of work.

The general purchasing power released for consumers by the reduced price should, however, be finding an outlet elsewhere, tending therefore to raise prices and profits in some other industry, and thus giving a similar though opposite indication that further investment of capital and further employment of labour is desirable there. This briefly is how industrial changes have been brought about in a capitalist organisation. Changes in relative prices operating through changes in relative profits act as indicators to capitalists, showing where it is desirable to increase the investment of capital and where it is desirable to check it.

The practical conclusion suggested by this brief analysis of the profit mechanism is that stability is impossible in a progressive economy unless capitalists encourage the production of those things which are likely to be relatively profitable, and discourage the production of those things which are likely to be relatively unprofitable. It is no use increasing production in industries where profits are relatively low, for low profits mean that production there has already gone far enough. It cannot of course be maintained that the real economy in which we live conforms at all closely to the ideal picture suggested by an analysis of sensitive responses to relative price and profit fluctuations. Some of the influences which check such prompt and sensitive responses, monopoly control and the like, are the commonplaces of a study of applied economics, and it is not necessary to elaborate them here. It is our task rather to deal with the peculiar difficulties which prevent the smooth functioning of the price and profit mechanism, when faced with the necessity for such adaptations as material progress demands.

Reluctance to admit the necessity for slowing down

the rate of agricultural development and facilitating the introduction of new supplies of labour into "tertiary" occupations clearly means a refusal to apply this fundamental rule of capitalist economy. It has repeatedly been made a matter of complaint in recent years that the industries which on the average are worst off are often those which are producing the basic necessities of life, and concerning the justification for whose existence there cannot be the slightest doubt, while the relatively prosperous industries are those engaged in supplying satisfactions which according to some standards are of doubtful real value, and which could easily be dispensed with, without inflicting any serious inconvenience upon anyone. The fact that the basic industries are relatively depressed while some of the others are doing well is an indication that the transfer of capital and labour, in accordance with increased productive capacity, from the former group of occupations to the latter, has not been carried through sufficiently rapidly.[1] The application of the rules of a capitalist economy shows that we need an expansion of employment, not in the basic industries, but in the industries which supply the means for satisfying our less important needs. The fact that the former are very depressed creates a strong presumption that there are

---

[1] According to Pigou (*Economic Journal*, September 1927, p. 356), had unemployment in Great Britain been due to any substantial extent to maldistribution of labour, "we should have expected to find a marked shortage of labour in important groups of industries to balance the excess in engineering, shipbuilding and so on; and of such marked shortage there is no sign". But it is surely impossible to defend the view that the great inequalities which exist between the values of different kinds of work, inequalities moreover which are bolstered up by a wide variety of devices for limiting the number of competitors, are not a *prima facie* proof of marked shortage of the more highly paid types of work. Apparent absence of demand for "tertiary" products may merely mean that those who to-day control their sale expect too high a price for them.

still relatively too many people employed in them. The only permanently satisfactory method that has ever been discovered for diminishing unemployment in a capitalist society is the encouragement of people to enter occupations and industries which are a little more prosperous than the average. The fact that public policy to-day is so generally designed to bring about results exactly the opposite of this shows how little the principles of a capitalist economy are understood even by those who profess themselves to be its most ardent adherents.

CHAPTER IV

MATERIAL PROGRESS AND INDIVIDUAL LOSSES

AT first sight the suggestion that it is wise to invest savings in the industries which are likely to be the most profitable seems so platitudinous as scarcely to require elaborate exposition. Rather, the thesis that there is a chronic tendency in certain circumstances to direct investment policy along other lines and that this tendency threatens to cause serious dislocations seems to call for explanation and defence. We are in fact arguing, first, that in a progressive economy general prosperity is unattainable unless there is a sufficient flow of capital into the industries which progress is making more profitable, and away from the industries which progress is making less profitable; and second, that capitalists as a group are unwilling to allow this flow. To many, in spite of the striking evidence afforded by the eager efforts to expand shipbuilding, the second proposition will seem highly paradoxical. Investment of this kind, it may be supposed, is likely to be profitable. It is the essential characteristic of the capitalist to look for profitable investments. Why then should it be suggested that he will refuse to act according to his nature? Is it in fact true that the capitalist is ignorant of the first principles of the system which it is his peculiar function to work?[1] It is one of our main tasks to explain this

[1] Instances are not lacking where the capitalist has been deliberately urged to ignore the canons of capitalist economy and continue un-

apparent paradox. If there is chronic under-production of the goods and services which a rapidly progressing economy needs, why do not some far-seeing capitalists set to work to produce these goods and services, thereby increasing their own incomes and at the same time conferring substantial benefits upon the society of which they are members?

A complete answer to this question will be long and complex, but it will be convenient to summarise here two of the most important parts of the answer, the central ideas of which can then be kept in mind throughout the more detailed discussion which is to follow.

The first partial answer to the question is that in fact capitalists do make investments of the right kind, but they do not make enough of them. The alternatives facing a capitalist are inadequately described if we think only of the simple choice between a profitable and an unprofitable investment. No capitalist, even the most short-sighted, would deliberately choose an investment which he knew to be unprofitable. The alternatives which face him are in fact very numerous. Some offer a small return and almost complete absence of risk—others a moderate return with a small degree of risk, while a third group, which itself contains an almost infinite number of variants, offers the prospect of very large returns combined with very considerable risk. Equilibrium in the economy as a whole demands an appropriate distribution of capital between the various groups of investment. Waste will

profitable production. In a survey of Australian policy during the depression, the *Sydney Morning Herald*, for example, rejoiced, *inter alia*, at "the faith of the farmer in continuing to produce unprofitable crops" (August 6, 1934).

result if too much capital goes into risky enterprises, and at certain stages of the history of the last century this error may have been important; there will, however, also be waste if insufficient capital is allowed for the more risky enterprises, and prolonged persistence in this error is quite possible without a single capitalist ever deliberately deciding in favour of an unprofitable investment, or indeed making a decision which could reasonably be condemned, if it could be assumed that some other investors were deciding differently.

Secondly, and probably more important, while it will be profitable for a capitalist to invest part of his savings in the type of enterprise which material progress demands, such investment will be highly distasteful to those capitalists who are already operating there, and who are anxious to avoid the risk of diminished income which is threatened by inconvenient competition. By various devices they attempt to check the inward flow of competing capital, so that even if there is a high degree of willingness on the part of other people to take the risks associated with the new types of enterprise, this willingness has no effect on the flow of capital. It is, as we said, the essential characteristic of the capitalist in general to look for profitable investments, but as often as not it is a characteristic of particular capitalists, and even more so of capitalists organised in groups, to protect the value of the investments which they have made in the past. The search for new profitable investments and the protection of old ones often lead to diametrically opposed policies.

If we approach the problem in a more general way, the central fact to be borne in mind in seeking an explanation of the apparent paradox of the capitalist refusing to act according to his nature is that material progress threatens loss to important groups of individuals, who accordingly take such steps as they consider will be effective to protect themselves against such loss. An analysis of these losses must therefore occupy a central place in any realistic study of a progressive economy.

In the first place, and most obviously, individuals who have become accustomed to the performance of certain kinds of work, who have gone to some trouble in acquiring valuable skill and experience, are threatened with serious loss if a situation arises in which they are compelled to look for some new kind of work where their skill and experience no longer have any value.[1]

Experimentation in new fields of production is usually risky, and both labourers and capitalists fear that, if they make the plunge, they may lose everything. They are likely to have little clear idea of the nature of the new work which is needed, and naturally doubt whether in its performance they will be able to enjoy the same income as that which they have been in the habit of receiving. This risk itself has two different, though closely related, aspects. There are the uncertain risks associated with the new type of work or investment, but also there are the certain losses associated

---

[1] "The peculiarities of labour in relation to readjustments form one of the main sources of injustice and hardship in an individualist economy" (Knight, *Risk, Uncertainty, and Profit*, p. 346). The development of new methods of work sometimes displaces labour indirectly as well as directly. "The gas industry", the *Manchester Guardian Commercial* reported on September 30, 1933, "could have no finer testimonial than that paid at the opening of the British Commercial Gas Association at Bournemouth. A deputation of sweeps saw Sir Francis Goodenough, and asked him to arrange for alternative employment for their sons, as the extending use of gas fires made the living of a chimney sweep extremely precarious."

with the abandonment of the old. The latter are especially obvious in the case of the capitalist who is asked to acknowledge the fact that technical improvements have rendered superfluous some of the capital which has been invested in the older industries. His capital, and the capital of those from whom he has borrowed, is already tied up in an enterprise the abandonment of which may mean complete financial ruin, which neither he nor his creditors are willing to contemplate. None of us enjoys being disturbed, and the dismay of the average worker, who sees his employment disappearing, is only equalled by the dismay of the average capitalist, who sees the value of the capital which he has invested in some industry diminishing. It is scarcely surprising that both these groups are ready to take energetic steps, by government intervention or otherwise, to protect themselves against the necessity for change. The indifference with which capitalist society has contemplated the sacrifice of individuals ruthlessly pushed aside in the path of material progress constitutes indeed one of the most formidable indictments which can be levelled against it. A coal-miner is, it seems, being asked to abandon his skill as a coal-miner and try his fortune as, say, a musician, a type of work for which he has neither interest nor aptitude. A wheat farmer is asked to cut his capital losses in wheat-farming, and invest such new savings as he can scrape together in, say, a highly speculative aviation concern. Many a farmer has said that he would be quite willing to give up farming if he could only see some way of retrieving the money which he has sunk in his farm. Naturally he dislikes the prospect of change and prefers to believe that by some skilful manipulation of marketing or of credit policy he can save his capital and continue to make his farm pay. Reluctance to admit the necessity for change will be all the greater if he has others dependent upon him and realises keenly his responsibility for their welfare. "If he followed the instructions of the economists he might indeed be a better member of the great society, but he would probably be a worse husband and father." [1] Progress is thus likely to inflict loss upon people who have already invested capital in the older fields of industry, and they are willing to take desperate measures to protect the vested interests which have grown up, refusing to admit the inevitable losses which the writing down of obsolete capital plant would involve.[2] It was reported early in 1934 that ricksha-men in Chinkiang, on the Yangtsze River, resenting the introduction of a motor-bus service which threatened to ruin their livelihood, had engaged in vigorous rioting and completely smashed the bus company's fleet of vehicles. To a greater or less extent, as has been aptly said, we all share the mentality of the Chinkiang ricksha-man; the technique of sabotage adopted in more "advanced" societies is usually less crude, though not necessarily less effective.

The most dramatic transfers which material progress demands are of course transfers of labour. The problem of the drift to the towns, for example, is naturally visualised in terms of men and women abandoning farm work and taking up urban occupations. Similarly, we are familiar with the difficulty of transferring miners

---

[1] Barbara Wootton, *Plan or No Plan*, p. 159.

[2] Cf. the discussion on the question whether in the United States "business recovery is not being delayed by an all too general tendency to endeavor to maintain intact all of the various obligations and balance-sheet valuations of the Coolidge era of prosperity" (O. W. M. Sprague, *Recovery and Common Sense*, p. 84). See also G. L. Wood, *The Costs of Progress*, Melbourne University Press, 1934.

from industries where they are no longer wanted to some other field. The effects of resistance to change on the part of wage-earners are well known, and the foolishness of the labourer's resistance to the installation of more efficient methods of production is a commonplace of the economic historian. It must certainly be granted that greater individual capacity for prompt adaptation to changing circumstances would be a powerful aid in avoiding depression and in accelerating the rate of material progress. But it would be unreasonable to place too much responsibility upon the shoulders of labourers. The continued depression of coal-mining is not to any important extent due to the reluctance of coal-miners to seek other occupations. A diversion of the stream of capital is as necessary as a diversion of labour. In practice the most important person is the man who must take the first step, and he is usually the man who controls capital. It is from this point of view that the claim sometimes made on behalf of the capitalist that he "provides employment" has a certain validity. At the same time the admission of this claim clearly places a heavy responsibility upon him.

The losses with which individuals are threatened by material progress are not, however, solely of this kind. So far we have considered only losses inflicted upon people who formerly were associated with the older industries, either as workers or as capitalists. But those who are already engaged in the new fields of work feel that they too will suffer loss if the inward flow of competitors is not checked.

Many of the newer types of work are likely to be offering incomes well above the average, and any additional flow of labour into these fields is resisted because it threatens the differential advantages hitherto enjoyed by those fortunate enough to occupy quasi-monopolistic positions. This type of resistance is offered both by people who receive their incomes as a result of the performance of work and by capitalists. It can in fact be most conveniently studied in terms of the outlook of professional organisations. As one of the motives for monopoly development, it is already a well-known factor in the analysis of economic production. Actually it goes much deeper than this. Quite apart from any formal attempt to build up a monopoly organisation, both capitalists and labourers in privileged positions take all sorts of steps to protect their privileges. The dislocating effects of these efforts are all the more important to-day when the necessity for rapid adjustment has become so much more urgent.

Resistance to change is partly due to mere stupidity, reinforced by the effects of an attractive but delusive metaphor. Unfortunately, however, there is a good deal more in the problem than this. The pressure of more efficient competitors outside is certain to mean some loss of capital equipment. Vested interests, industrial, commercial and financial, which feel themselves intimately bound up with the maintenance of the value of this capital equipment, will do all in their power to prevent action which seems likely to compel them to face their losses squarely and write down their capital. In many instances, in the long run, their efforts must fail, but in the meantime they are most effective in inflicting losses on other people. The resistance of the small man, who sees himself faced with complete ruin is natural enough, and it is impossible to deny him a considerable measure of sympathy, and perhaps too of other things which he will value more than sympathy, but the resistance of the big man is just as desperate and much more dangerous. In effect, the root of the problem is that people who at any given stage of industrial development find themselves in a position which offers them an income and the privileges associated with income much above the average level of the rest of the community are prepared to oppose vigorously any policy which is necessary for moving to the next stage of development, if it seems likely to endanger their privileges and to reduce their incomes, either absolutely or in comparison with the incomes of other people.

If we press this line of argument further, we shall discover at least a partial justification for the belief that competition for limited markets threatens war. Commercial interests which already have their capital tied up in equipment for supplying existing markets will resist any threat to their position which arises from the competition of new competitors. The position is, however, inaccurately described if it is represented that capitalists will want to fight because they are inevitably compelled to produce more goods than the markets can absorb. Actually they find difficulty in discovering sufficient new markets because they are all anxious to continue the production of the same old things. They persist in doing this, in part at least, because any radical change in the character of the goods produced is likely to inflict severe capital losses, and to render impossible the maintenance of long-cherished positions of privilege.

It has already been hinted that the losses which people enjoying privileged positions are likely to suffer in consequence of the readjustments which material progress demands are themselves of two kinds.

There are first the absolute losses registered when elements of monopoly income disappear, but there are also relative losses incurred when the position of other people lower in the income scale improves in such a way as to make improbable the continued performance of certain services at the customary low rates of pay. This point of view is well illustrated by the opinion once frankly expressed by a woman who said she did not want the average income-level to rise too much, because it would then become difficult for her to get anyone to do cheap day work looking after her garden. If during the next few decades the average standard of income were substantially raised, it is certain that drastic reorganisation of certain types of work would be necessary of a kind which would impose inconveniences not so much on those who have been in the habit of performing such work as on those who have been in the habit of purchasing it. It would, for example, be impossible to have domestic service performed at anything like the rates which are common to-day, and with numerous attractive openings for girls elsewhere in industry and commerce, many who were accustomed to employ domestic servants would find it increasingly difficult to pay the prevailing rates of pay which the new circumstances would make appropriate; some revolutionary reorganisation of domestic work would accordingly become necessary. There are few who would care to affirm in set terms that material progress should be checked lest the supply of cheap domestic service should be endangered. When, however, we remember the reasons which led a New Zealand Minister of the Crown only a few years ago to express doubts about the wisdom of further extensions of secondary education, it is difficult to believe that this attitude of mind is entirely without influence. If everybody received a secondary education, "who, then", he asked, "would do the dirty work?" The undisguised satisfaction evinced in certain quarters at the increased difficulties which recent economies in educational expenditure threaten to place in the way of children of poor parents training for work better paid than that which their parents had been able to offer also shows that this sentiment of class-distinction is an important factor in the situation.

If we left our analysis of the losses which material progress is likely to inflict upon individuals at this stage, we should still, however, have neglected certain vital factors. For it would apparently still be open to us to maintain that, while the selfish desire to protect traditional income standards revealed a point of view which no doubt merited severe criticism, its economic significance was perhaps not so serious, if it meant merely some slowing down of the rate of material progress. After all, it might be claimed, while it must be admitted that rising levels of real income were a good, it was even more true that a high degree of instability was an evil, for the avoidance of which we might reasonably make some material sacrifice. To determine the validity of this claim, we must examine not only the losses which material progress inflicts upon individuals, but also the losses which are inflicted by resistance to the adaptations which are demanded.

The losses inflicted upon the individuals who are deprived of the opportunity of rising to higher income-levels are obvious enough, and no more need be said about them. In addition, however, it will be argued below that resistance to adaptation threatens to disturb the equilibrium of the whole economy so that losses are inflicted even on those individuals who have resisted progress in order to protect their own privileged positions. If this is so, the individual losses which have already been discussed cannot in the long run be avoided by refusing to make the necessary adaptations. If the objective conditions exist which make rapid material progress possible, the effective choice before us is not the attainment of this goal, on the one hand, with risks of individual insecurity, and on the other, slow or no progress, combined with stability for individuals. We must in fact choose between progress and retrogression; if we deliberately prefer stability to progress, we shall before long find that we have sacrificed both.

In discussing the theory that persistent refusal to make the diversions of labour and capital from less remunerative to more remunerative industries which material progress demands will create a chronic tendency to depression throughout the whole field of industry, we touch upon the theory of repercussions which has played such an important part in recent discussions, both academic and popular, of business fluctuations.[1] In one sense or another, it is true that there are few sections of economic theory which are not concerned with repercussions of some kind. We are always endeavouring to trace out the general con-

[1] Cf. Pigou, *Industrial Fluctuations*, esp. Book I. chs. iv., v., ix.; *Theory of Unemployment*, esp. Part III. ch. xii.; D. H. Robertson, *A Study of Industrial Fluctuations*, pp. 125-55, 165-70; E. R. Walker, *Australia in the World Depression*, pp. 160-68; J. M. Keynes, *The Means to Prosperity*, ch. ii.; R. F. Kahn, "The Relation of Home Investment to Unemployment", *Economic Journal*, June 1931; L. F. Giblin, *Australia*, 1930; W. L. Valk, "Relation between Partial Overproduction and General Depression", and R. Frisch, "Propagation Problems and Impulse Problems in Dynamic Economics", in *Economic Essays* in honour of Gustav Cassel.

sequences for the economic structure as a whole of changes in some given part of it. Here, however, we are more interested in the more modest task of estimating the significance for the whole economy of a condition of unusual prosperity or unusual depression in some single industry or group of industries, whatever may have been the originating cause of prosperity or depression, and in particular, in the consequences of persistent over-production in industries in which technical improvements have occurred and for whose products demand is inelastic. Such over-production will create depression in the industries which are immediately affected. Is there any reason for supposing that this depression will be transmitted to other industries? If we refuse to make the transfers of labour and capital which are required, our economy is one in which the appropriate proportions between the various kinds of production are deliberately not maintained, and it is desirable to develop a theory which will explain the general consequences of such a decision. The indications which the movements of the relative price and profit mechanism give to producers are ignored. What consequences are likely to be observed in an economy subject to chronic and deliberate errors of this kind?

The orthodox abstract analysis of economic theory has usually been based on the "assumption that the positive and negative errors of judgment on the part of entrepreneurs will, on the average and apart from monetary disturbances, cancel out".[1] Such errors are, in the statistical phrase, random errors; they are as likely to be in one direction as in the other, and therefore in the long run their combined effects might safely

---

[1] E. F. M. Durbin, *Purchasing Power and Trade Depression*, p. 74 n.

be neglected. The errors which are likely to be made, when we are faced with the necessity for adapting ourselves to potential increases in production, are, however, not of this random kind. If some entrepreneurs over-estimate what the market is able to absorb, while others under-estimate, the aggregate of production is in the end unlikely to be far wrong, but if, after all counterbalancing errors have been cancelled out, there still remains a larger number of entrepreneurs than is required, who insist on producing wheat, or boots, or steamships, the general effect of such "biassed" errors is clearly likely to be cumulative. Such errors are so common as to justify the attribution to them of the adjective "normal". Is it possible to make some general statement about their character and consequences?

The connection between technical progress and the trade cycle has often been emphasised. The whole of Cassel's theory of the trade cycle is in fact based on the view that it is an inevitable concomitant of technical progress.[1] Our thesis is somewhat different. Fluctuations in general business conditions are the consequence, it will be argued, not only of the processes of adaptation demanded by technical progress but also of persistent refusal to make the necessary adaptations.

Such a theory of investment error will enable us to see in better perspective the significance of the growing burden of debt to which so much attention has been paid in recent popular discussions. Apart from the influence of general deflationary price movements, debt becomes an insupportable burden only if the capital investment from which the debt liability has grown has been badly placed. If there were no investment errors, debt burdens would never become insupport-

[1] *Theory of Social Economy*, 1932 ed., pp. 642-8.

able, provided there were no serious deflationary price movements. Those who complain of debt burdens should direct their attention first to the causes of chronic errors in investment.

Economic literature has not indeed entirely neglected the discussion of an economy in which the normal canons of capitalist investment were abandoned. Cannan has pointed out that "if people with one accord left off doing what paid, we should all be dead in two months",[1] and Sir Josiah Stamp has discussed the risks of introducing "chaos, Bedlam and Laputa into the conduct of industry" by attempting to organise "a Society framed on the Extra Mile Principle". In such a society, it might be "agreed that whereas 5 per cent would be economically necessary to induce people to refrain from consuming and induce them to save and subscribe to industry, they should actually be Christian enough to do it for 4 per cent, and that everyone desiring capital should be generous enough not to screw lenders down to the 5 per cent that they could secure it for on lines of degrading economic competition, but should offer 6 per cent. Every worker instead of looking at the clock at five should think only of others and work till six, every employer, instead of expecting work until five o'clock, as economic conditions would demand, agreed to let them go at four o'clock, or instead of paying the economic wages for which he could secure a worker, gave by common consent 10 per cent more."[2] Such a society from which the profit motive had disappeared would clearly demand drastic reorganisation in all sorts of ways which well-intentioned people have not appreciated.

[1] *Economic Outlook*, p. 176.
[2] *The Christian Ethic as an Economic Factor*, p. 57.

The more important practical problems arise, however, not when we completely abandon the profit criterion, but when we apply it partially, or with imperfect understanding of the indications which the profit mechanism gives us. It is unlikely that people will with one accord leave off doing what pays, but when circumstances change so that what once paid is no longer profitable, it is highly probable that they will refuse to recognise this fact, and will insist upon doing what does not pay. When this happens, a theory of investment error is needed to supplement the theory which assumes on the average correct decisions on the part of investors.

The possibility of investment error has played a large and important part in discussions of the business cycle. Especially under the influence of Pigou, the effect of cumulative errors of optimism or of pessimism is widely admitted as an important influence, which, if it does not directly generate industrial fluctuations, at least intensifies the effects of other causes. The errors to which attention is now being directed are, however, of a different kind. Pigou's errors of optimism and pessimism are, so to speak, general errors, unduly expanding or unduly contracting investment of all kinds. The errors now under discussion are errors of judgment, errors in discriminating between investment in different industries. Whether there is too much or too little investment in general, there is also, it is argued, a chronic tendency to over-investment in certain industries, relative to other industries, and our task is to analyse the general effects of this chronic tendency upon the stability of the whole economy.

Whatever we may eventually discover to be the

correct opinion upon this question, there is certainly a widespread belief that depression in any single industry is likely to infect other industries, causing a general slackening of industrial activity, or what comes to the same thing, that complete recovery from depression in any industry is dependent upon similar recovery in other industries. Bagehot expounded the popular view in a well-known passage (*Lombard Street*, pp. 121-2). "No single large industry can be depressed without injury to other industries; still less can any great group of industries. Each industry when prosperous buys and consumes the produce of many other industries, and if industry A fails or is in difficulty, industries B, and C, and D, which used to sell to it, will not be able to sell that which they had produced in reliance on A's demand, and in future they will stand idle till industry A recovers, because in default of A there will be none to buy the commodities which they create. Then as industry B buys of C, D, etc., the adversity of B tells on C, D, etc., and as these buy of E, F, etc., the effect is propagated through the whole alphabet." If improved methods, for example, greatly increase the world's supplies of wheat or of sugar or of butter, but wheat and dairy farmers and sugar producers are everywhere steadfastly unanimous in refusing to abandon their customary occupations, and continue to pour forth upon a satiated world increasing supplies of their products, the prices of these things naturally tend to fall far below the level to which the improvements in production, reflected in lower costs, would have brought them. The diminished incomes of the producers concerned will result in a diminished demand for other things, the prices of which will accordingly tend to fall as well. Similarly, unusual prosperity among any important group of producers, farmers, for example, will, it is believed, be transmitted to other groups. Farmers will have more to spend, and their increased demand will drive up other prices, thus encouraging greater activity in other industries.

This simple analysis, in terms of monetary purchasing power, is, however, unsatisfactory and it fails to establish the point towards which it is directed. The difficulty is closely related to that which we shall encounter later in attempts to solve the problem of technological unemployment in terms of purchasing power. Producers in the over-developed industries will, it is true, have smaller incomes, but purchasers of their products will at the same time have additional purchasing power released with which they can purchase other things. The producers' loss of income is balanced by this released purchasing power, and the aggregate of purchasing power appears to remain unchanged. It is not true, as Bagehot maintained, that industries B, C and D must stand idle till A recovers, "because in default of A, there will be no one to buy the commodities which they create". Because A's products are cheaper, producers in B, C and D, etc., who are in the habit of buying A's products will have more to spend on other things, and can therefore buy more of each other's products.

If the argument is developed in Bagehot's simple terms, it is apparently impossible to show that depression in one industry will have generally depressing effects upon industry as a whole. It is true that the additional purchasing power which producers in B, C and D now have at their disposal may not be expended in precisely the same way as the purchasing power lost by producers in A would have been used. Instead of buying more of each other's products, they may prefer to buy the products of X, Y and Z, but that would merely mean depression in certain industries combined with unusual prosperity in others. It would not, by itself, cause a general depression everywhere.

Are we then compelled to conclude that the whole theory of repercussions as set out by Bagehot and to which ordinary experience appears to lend so much support must be abandoned? Two general considerations require attention before we give an affirmative answer to this question. In expounding the opposite process, the repercussions of prosperity, it is now generally admitted that any statement of the problem in terms of purchasing power is inadequate. If as a result of increased demand for its products, or because greater efficiency makes it possible to offer cheaper goods which elicit an elastic demand, any industry becomes more prosperous, a simple discussion in terms of purchasing power seems to suggest that the additional demand which is diverted to the prosperous industry must be withdrawn from other industries which accordingly would be depressed. This is so obviously contrary to general experience that a further examination of the facts is necessary. Depression in other industries can be avoided only if the additional demand for the products of the prosperous industry is not merely a transferred demand, but is actually a net addition to the aggregate demand already in existence, and this will not happen unless other industries at the same time expand their own output. General prosperity will be the result of prosperity in a particular industry, only if producers in other fields are stimulated to greater efforts by the possibility of getting a bigger supply of the cheap products of the prosperous industry, and accordingly expand their output too. Pigou and Robertson have accordingly discussed the problem of repercussions as depending upon the elasticity of consumers' demand for the products of a prosperous industry, measured in terms of the effort which they themselves are willing to make.[1] If the products of any industry become cheaper and more plentiful, potential purchasers who are at work in other industries will be stimulated to greater activity so that they will be able to place more of their own products upon the market and thereby assure to themselves not only increased supplies of the cheaper goods but the same supplies as before of other things. The prosperity of any single industry has repercussions of a favourable kind upon other industries because such reactions actually occur.

A consideration of the circumstances of a primitive society in which barter is the general rule shows that this view has at least some validity. If one group is producing wheat, another cloth and a third housing equipment, anything which made it possible for the wheat-producers to offer larger supplies of wheat in exchange for cloth and furniture might also stimulate the cloth-makers to greater efforts so that they could buy more wheat without diminishing their demand for furniture. In more highly developed societies, where there is complex division of labour, and the entrepreneur-wage-earner relationship has a predominating influence, similar reactions no doubt sometimes occur. The decision to increase production usually, however,

---

[1] Pigou, *Industrial Fluctuations*, pp. 63 *et seq.*; Robertson, *Study of Industrial Fluctuations*, p. 125.

rests with a few individuals who themselves may be little affected directly by the cheaper products of the prosperous industry. A reduction of costs in any industry will give entrepreneurs in other industries a strong stimulus to expand their own activities only on the hypothesis that as soon as the prices of the things purchased by wage-earners begin to fall, money wages are immediately reduced. Such delicate and speedy adjustment of wages would tend to increase the entrepreneur's margin of profit, and this would encourage him to increase his output. This hypothesis is, however, usually somewhat remote from the real world. It is difficult therefore to believe that the simple considerations which are effective in a primitive community have much importance in a modern industrial society. In practice it seems more probable that decisions to increase output are made independently in different industries for a wide variety of reasons, and that repercussions from the prosperity of other industries are seldom directly effective for this purpose.

We are, however, more concerned with repercussions which originate in depression. Discussion in terms of the elasticity of consumers' demand, in terms of the effort which they are willing to make to increase their effective demand, would here lead to some such results as the following. By hypothesis, consumers do not wish to spend so much as before on the products of the depressed industry. The ease with which they are now able to get all they need then leads them to slacken their efforts, and output falls off all round. Again, in a primitive society we can see that such a sequence of events is possible. If wheat were already so abundantly supplied that demand for it was highly inelastic, any considerable increase in its quantity which compelled wheat-producers to offer more wheat for the same quantity of cloth or furniture might cause the cloth-makers to slacken in their work and reduce their production, thus diminishing the average level of real income. In modern industrial societies, however, anything of this kind appears to be highly improbable. Producers in general will go on producing as in the past until the failure of demand makes it impossible to sell their whole output. It is difficult to conceive of circumstances in which their efforts would relax, because they found that they could get the products of a depressed industry more cheaply than before. This attempt to get behind the theory of repercussions in terms of purchasing power, therefore, does not help us much in explaining the probable course of events when there is persistent over-production of some staple commodity.

In the second place, however, the purchasing power theory may be criticised on account of the assumption that any additional purchasing power which the consumers of cheap goods find at their disposal will always be immediately converted, without any time-lag, into effective demand. Instead of spending the released purchasing power available for producers of B, C and D, as a result of the fall in the price of A, consumers may for a time slow down their rate of expenditure. There is likely to be some delay in deciding what new things are to be purchased, and the effects of this delay will be intensified by the alarms of the people in A who on account of depression will feel disposed to conserve their resources. The effects of diminished purchasing power are felt by producers in A immediately, but the effects of released purchasing power elsewhere may be suspended for a sufficient period of time to initiate a general depression of industry. This will be especially important when there is any considerable time-lag between the receipt of lower incomes by producers and the purchase of cheap products by consumers. If the price of wool falls, this will ultimately no doubt be reflected in cheaper woollen clothing, but the cheaper clothing may not be available for many months, and in the meantime the released purchasing power, or part of it, is held in suspense by one or other of the numerous intermediaries between primary producer and final consumer, who are unlikely to treat these temporary accumulations as income.[1] If the price of only one commodity has fallen, the general repercussions may be negligible, but where technical improvements are numerous, the consequences of temporary hoarding may be very serious, setting in motion a distinctly deflationary trend.

It has also been argued [2] that we can reject the repercussion theory only on the impossible assumption of a prompt and smooth adaptation of productive resources which will provide immediately an adequate supply of the new things upon which the released purchasing power is likely to be expended. Unless there is available a large reservoir of unused resources which can at once be diverted to the production of the additional goods which are eventually demanded, there may be considerable delay in changing the forms in

---

[1] Cf. H. V. Hodson, *Economics of a Changing World*, pp. 105-6. Falling prices, even if confined to one part only of the economic structure of a country, induce in producers and merchants, even to some extent in final consumers, a reluctance to spend, and therefore cause a reduction of the velocity of circulation, or delay in spending the incomes created by former prices, according to the method of analysis favoured. There is always a lag in the transference of any part of a fixed volume of spending power from one kind of purchasable thing to another, and the psychological and practical mischief may be done during the period of that lag.

[2] Cf. W. L. Valk, *loc. cit.*

which capital and labour are already crystallised. In fact the only way in which an adequate supply of new resources could be obtained might be by a diversion from the depressed and over-developed industries, and by hypothesis it is this diversion which is being resisted, the over-developed industry insisting upon using all the resources at its command to keep up the volume of output. So long as this attitude is maintained, it is impossible to get the appropriate expansion of other industries, upon which the re-establishment of equilibrium must depend. This point is central in the whole of our argument, but at this stage it does not help much to explain the repercussions which depressed industries are likely to have upon industry in general. If the expansion of relatively new industries is hampered by the difficulty of getting adequate supplies of labour and capital, those already engaged in such industries will nevertheless be prosperous because the supply of their products will not be quickly adapted to the growing demand, and prices and profits will therefore be high. We should again be faced with a combination of depressed and prosperous industries and not with general depression. Apart from the effects of credit policy, which have so far been ignored, the time-lag which intervenes before consumers convert into effective demand the purchasing power which is released when they buy the cheap products of depressed industries is the most important channel through which the effects of depression in one industry are transmitted to other industries. Nor is it a matter merely of waiting till demand becomes effective. Especially where a large number of industries are concerned, the time-lag may be sufficiently long to set in motion other depressing forces the effects of which cannot be reversed merely by the decision of consumers to spend their temporary hoards.

In our discussion of the time-lag which slows down the rate of expenditure, we have already been dealing with a problem of credit, but we have throughout assumed that conscious or deliberate variations in credit policy may be neglected. When, however, we remove the somewhat unreal hypothesis that banking policy is likely to be neutral in its effects, the case for believing that persistent partial over-production will lead to general depression is much strengthened. The appropriate credit policy in the face of partial over-production is an offer of credit on more liberal terms for use in relatively under-developed industries. Technological improvements reduce costs. If prices then are lowered, there should be a reduced demand for credit because less credit will be needed to finance the sale of the same volume of goods. Some credit will accordingly be released or set free, which should be available for new uses, and by means of this released credit the displaced labour can be reabsorbed.[1] This argument does not seem to call for credit expansion in the ordinary sense, but merely for the maintenance of the volume of credit at the old level. Some credit formerly advanced to the old industries is no longer needed there, and can therefore, without any change in general credit policy, be transferred to the new. But from the point of view which credit institutions are likely to adopt, the maintenance of the volume of credit, depending as it would, on a reduction in the interest rate, would look very much like credit expansion, and there might be some hesitation in permitting such a thing. So long as there was hesitation, the general effect of

[1] Cf. Hansen, *Economic Stabilization in an Unbalanced World*, ch. x.

credit policy would be deflationary. Moreover, if relative over-production occurred in industries which occupied a traditionally important place in the economy as a whole, the tendency towards excessive caution in credit policy would be all the stronger. The losses involved in writing off capital equipment which had become superfluous would fall in part upon the banks themselves, which would share the reluctance of the people actively engaged in depressed industries to face the fact of inevitable loss. Bankers, moreover, are as much liable as other people to the influence of the powerful complex of ideas which demands the maintenance of the *status quo* in the staple industries, and in these circumstances their policy, so far from accelerating the rate of adjustment, is likely to encourage still more over-production.

We have given reasons for rejecting the simpler kinds of reasoning whereby it has been thought possible to establish the thesis that depression in one industry will lead in ever-widening circles to further depression throughout the whole of the economy. But we have nevertheless attempted to reach much the same conclusion by another route. In the course of time, no doubt, there would be a tendency to return to equilibrium. Banking policy would adjust itself to the new conditions and the time-lag in consumers' expenditure would disappear. If one or more groups of producers stubbornly insisted upon continuing their work in conditions which offered them permanently subnormal returns, there is nothing in the nature of things to prevent the establishment of equilibrium in spite of this refusal to respond to narrowly economic stimuli. But in the process of adjustment, the economy is likely to encounter severe shocks, which may leave it unsteady for a long time.

It is not argued that this is the only, or indeed the most important, cause of trade depressions. The conclusion nevertheless appears to be justified that persistent refusal to make the transfers of labour and capital which material progress demands is likely ultimately to lead to a general depression in all industries and not merely to a depression in the industries where there is in the first instance chronic over-supply. If people in privileged positions persist in defending their privileges by excluding the competition of labour and capital which is no longer needed elsewhere, so that old-established industries are chronically over-developed, their own positions are likely ultimately to be undermined. They will lose the security which they so eagerly desire and will themselves be compelled to share the depression which they have inflicted upon others. Personal security is like happiness in that it is likely to elude a direct search. In a progressive economy, stability and personal security are to be found only as a by-product of the search for something else.

Individual and Social Costs of Change

The losses inflicted on individuals by industrial change, it has been said, are obviously real, but it has nevertheless been disputed whether these individual losses should be taken into account in measuring the net effects of any change and therefore in deciding whether the change is economic or not. Pigou says it is a mistake to include them separately, to argue that "the value of the marginal social net product of resources invested in developing 'new methods of production' is less than the value of the marginal private net product, because there is not included in the latter any allowance for the depreciation which the improvement causes in the value of existing plant".[1] The view which is commonly held that allowance for such depreciation should be made Pigou describes as "a somewhat specious fallacy", maintaining instead that "whatever loss the old producers suffer through a reduction in the price of their products is balanced by the gain which the reduction confers upon the purchasers of these products".[2] "There is no loss to the owners of the old machines, in respect of any unit of their former output, that is not offset by an equivalent gain to consumers."

Pigou's argument has been described as "a curious classicism",[3] which in any case "hardly meets the point that one man suffers damage in order that another may gain". Pigou argues that, if each claim that depreciation of existing plant should be taken into account in the estimate of net social gain from new methods of production were admitted, it "would justify the State in prohibiting the use of new machinery that dispenses with the services of skilled mechanics until the generation of mechanics possessing that skill has been depleted by death". But if the displaced skilled mechanic does not immediately find alternative employment, he has to be maintained somehow, and the costs of his maintenance cannot be ignored in estimating the net social gain from adopting the improved method. The problem can be approached from the point of view either of the losses inflicted on displaced labour or of

---

[1] *Economics of Welfare*, Part II. ch. viii. para. 10, 1929 ed., Pt. II. ch. ix. para. 11.

[2] Cf. M. Bouniatian, "Technical Progress and Unemployment", *International Labour Review*, March 1933, p. 342.

[3] M. A. Copeland, "Communities of Interest and the Price System", *Trend of Economics*, pp. 141-4.

the losses inflicted on the owners of displaced capital. The principles involved can, however, be considered most conveniently from the angle of the displaced labourer. Copeland suggests two analogies. Until recently, in most countries, the depreciation of labourers through senescence has not fallen on the employer, and consequently he has sometimes been too ready to dispense with old workers because he is not called upon to make any provision for their maintenance after dismissal. Similarly the advantages enjoyed from the importation of immigrants accustomed to low wages arises in part from the fact that the employers who purchase their services do not have to carry the costs of maintaining the men displaced by the immigrants. To both of these analogies Pigou no doubt would answer that, although the losses of the displaced labourers in both cases are real, from the point of view of the net social product as a whole their losses are offset by other people's gains. Put roughly, the results of technological improvements, according to those who think allowances should be made for the depreciation of displaced factors of production, are to be measured by the gain to the investor, minus the loss to the displaced labourer or the owner of the displaced capital. As against this Pigou argues that the results are gain to the investor, plus gain for consumers from lower prices, minus loss to displaced labourers or the owners of displaced capital, and the last two, he maintains, cancel out.[1]

Pigou's position is not entirely satisfactory. The corollary about the displaced skilled mechanic is wrong, because if the displaced mechanic can find other employment his maintenance involves no additional

[1] Cf. Sir Josiah Stamp, "Must Science Ruin Economic Progress", *Hibbert Journal*, April 1934, pp. 395-7.

social cost. There is no cost to anyone if he at once finds employment in some new industry, which is opened up by the application of productive resources no longer needed elsewhere. If, however, such absorption is long delayed, there is a real social cost which cannot be ignored. The whole difficulty arises from the fact that the purchasing and productive power released by technological improvements is not always made immediately effective. Entrepreneurs hesitate about new ventures, and are encouraged in their hesitation by a temporary satiety on the part of consumers. The weakness of Pigou's position arises from the fact that he seems to ignore the difficulties of the transition period. His argument appears to suggest that there is nothing to choose, from the standpoint of net social gain, between an invention which displaces a labourer who can immediately find employment elsewhere, and one which displaces a labourer whose skill is so specialised that prompt re-employment is impossible, and this conclusion is clearly difficult to defend. Copeland's criticisms of Pigou, on the other hand, do not adequately take into account the possibilities or the conditions of reabsorbing the displaced labour, appearing to assume that displacement is final and irrevocable.[1]

[1] The question discussed here arises in a specially interesting way with regard to improvements in transport. In regulating motor traffic, should we take into account the depreciation of the railways? Pigou's answer to this question is in effect, No! The losses of railway capital are offset by the advantages conferred upon consumers by the lower costs of transport. The fact that railways are able to adopt a price-policy based upon discriminating monopoly, however, suggests some doubts about the validity of this answer. Motor competition will compel a reduction in the price of some railway services, more particularly of high-rated traffic, but on account of the existence of discriminating monopoly, this reduction is likely to be accompanied by a rise in the price of other railway products, where motor competition is not effective, so that the gain which those consumers enjoy, who use the services where motor

These considerations raise the further question which Pigou also discusses whether the risk of loss through obsolescence may not increase the reluctance of business men to make investment in new plant which is liable to have its earnings reduced at short notice by new inventions. He agrees that this is probable, but also points out that further improvements are not likely to be discovered, unless opportunities are given for new methods to be actually tried out, so that on balance a competitive system which ignores the losses inflicted on those who use the old methods is likely to give better results. There is no doubt much force in this contention, but it does not diminish the significance of the more fundamental issue which we are pressing. Risks of loss are likely on the whole to increase when the importance of rapid obsolescence increases, as it is doing in modern highly capitalised industries. These risks will be taken more seriously if for other reasons the advantages of individual stability are being valued more highly. Capitalists as a whole then become more and more reluctant to take risks, refuse to do anything which is likely to compel them to face the hard facts of obsolescence, and capital is poured in excessive quantities into investments which are apparently safe. There is a fundamental conflict between the demands of material progress and the individual capitalist's desire for personal security.[1]

competition is effective, is offset by the losses of other consumers. It is possible that considerations of this kind are equally important in other fields. Nor can we neglect as insignificant the distinction between the cases where capital loss is definitely concentrated on a few people, and can be immediately compulsorily liquidated, and the case of State-owned railways where the loss cannot be liquidated in this way but remains a perpetual taxation burden.

[1] This discussion also suggests another interesting side issue. Are improvements in technique likely to be made more promptly by

monopolists or by freely competing firms? It is sometimes suggested and with some reason that monopolists will be more efficient in prompt adoption of new methods, as they have no inducement to conceal such improvements as have been discovered, and they will be ready to apply them quickly to all the units of production under their control. It is true that if the decision to try out a new method has been made, a monopoly will make such a decision effective over a wide field more rapidly than would competing producers; monopolists may, however, be unduly slow in making the decision in favour of new methods. Because the loss of displaced capital is theirs, as well as the gain from the new methods, they will be more cautious than competing units would be in adopting new inventions. Competing units would not need to concern themselves about the depreciation or displacement of their rivals' capital equipment. Cf. Pigou's discussion of the attitude of Government enterprises to new inventions: *Economics of Welfare*, 1929 ed., Book II. ch. xxii. para. 11 (old ed. pp. 391-5).

CHAPTER V

(i) *The Inevitability of Transfers*

WE cannot avoid the difficulties raised by the problems
of transfer merely by denying that material progress
is worth while, and deciding that we will have none of
it, or that the rate of movement should be retarded.
Suppose that we despair of the possibility of making
the necessary changes and decide to abandon progress
in favour of a stationary economy. Have we then really
avoided our troubles? Faced with reluctance to move
on the part of capitalists and labourers, many politicians and publicists are apt to seek for solutions
which will make movement unnecessary. The search
for solutions of this kind is a search for a will-o'-the-
wisp, for something which does not exist.

If we were starting from a position of equilibrium,
the decision to abandon any hope of further material
progress might, provided that it were possible to check
any further movement in the growth of science, enable
us to avoid the necessity for any further adjustment.
But starting as we do to-day from a position of dis-
equilibrium, some difficult adjustments have in any
case to be made. The most obvious and probable
method of aiming at stability, and therefore of avoid-

ing inconvenient adjustments, is by further efforts in the direction of self-sufficiency. Efforts of this kind would, however, themselves make necessary just as many and as difficult changes as the attempt to adjust our organisation to conditions of freer international exchange. High tariffs will no doubt protect some factory operatives from the necessity for change, but they will upset just as many transport workers and farmers, so that on the whole there will be no net gain. If difficult adjustments are in any case necessary it seems more sensible to prefer those which will at the same time make possible a higher standard of living. And in any case, apart from the obvious folly of checking such growth, and refusing to exercise the widening control of our environment which the growth of science makes possible, it is impossible to visualise any effective method for imposing this policy of despair upon mankind. In discussing the adaptations which we have to make in the face of potential material progress, we are not discussing something about which we have much range in choice. Some adaptations must inevitably be made; our choice lies between making them foolishly and making them wisely.

Apart from any idea of insuring against the risks of change by a policy of autarchy, some countries may find some measure of self-sufficiency forced upon them by circumstances outside their control. If we assume that the tide of economic nationalism is too powerful to be stemmed, are the fundamental conclusions which we have drawn from our analysis of material progress affected, or are we faced merely with a change, though obviously a most important change, in the framework within which they are to be applied? This question has immediate practical importance for countries like

Australia and New Zealand, which are threatened by measures necessitating a reversal of the trend towards expansion of production of kinds which we have come to regard as normal. It is widely believed that the only possible reaction to policies of this kind is the encouragement of subsistence farming, whereby individuals or groups, at a low standard of living, can at least maintain themselves by consuming the labour of their own hands without any attempt to place upon the markets, which are already glutted, additional supplies of their produce.

The general argument against the acceptance of such counsels of despair has been elaborated earlier, but there is no reason why it should be accepted even in the most unfavourable circumstances, where trade contacts with the outside world have been reduced to the barest minimum. At the present time, the inhabitants of Australia and New Zealand are in the habit of purchasing and consuming supplies of A, B, C, D, E, etc.; they have produced much more of A and B than they need or desire to consume themselves, and as a consequence have been able to get their supplies of C and D by exchange for part of their output of A and B. The outlet for exports is now contracted, and they are therefore no longer able to get C and D by the normal processes of international trade. The problem then arises of finding for the resources no longer needed to produce the old supplies of A and B some alternative field of employment. To the extent to which the interruption of international trade lowers the average standard of living—and it must have some effect of this kind—it is probable that there will be some extension of farming which allows those who engage in it little more than a bare subsistence. But other courses are also open. It may be possible to produce a little of C and D at home; but even if this is not so, the violent upset in relative costs which the restrictions of external trade are certain to cause is likely to alter the order in which goods and services are placed in the consumers' schedule of relative valuations. The restriction of production of A and B sets free a certain volume of productive resources. Instead of nailing them down to industries which certainly do not need them, they should now be transferred to the production, say, of L, M and N, which were formerly unobtainable because C and D were cheap enough to absorb all the available purchasing power.

We may take as an extreme case a country which was entirely cut off from connections with the outside world. Such a country would have to content itself with a more modest standard of living than it could expect if it were part of a larger unit. Some commodities would disappear altogether from consumers' schedules of demand. But so long as the fundamental condition of increasing knowledge was operative there is no reason why, provided its citizens were willing to make adjustments and changes of the kind which have here been described, they too should not enjoy rising standards of living, rising no doubt at a rate slower than might be enjoyed if external links had not been broken and taking forms which in some respects might be very different from those enjoyed elsewhere, but still worth having and worth taking the trouble which the essential adjustments demanded. Even in a country upon which self-sufficiency is imposed, the organisation of the production of poetry and philosophy has more economic value than the increased production of goods which are already in abundant supply. The process of adjustment would undoubtedly be difficult and violent, but it would be no more difficult and violent than the adjustments which would be demanded by recourse to subsistence farming on an extensive scale.

It has already been pointed out that numerous labour transfers of the kind here indicated have occurred in the past and are in fact still occurring every day. The alleged southward drift of industry in England which has recently been much discussed is an illustration of this trend. In the past material progress has been a real thing and in its course many individuals have passed from one occupation to another. Some old industries have continued to flourish, others have decayed and been replaced by industries whose economic significance had been small, and in addition some entirely new industries have grown up. If producers in the nineteenth century had shown the same reluctance as producers are encouraged to show to-day to change the character of their work and investment, we should have had, on the one hand, still more damaging gluts of elemental food supplies, and of equipment for producing the simpler forms of manufactured goods, while on the other hand we should have had no motor-cars, no radio, no electric light or telephone, no photography, no popular press, no wireless, no cimena, no gramophones, and nothing of numerous other goods and services which we take for granted to-day and the production of which provides employment for a substantial proportion of the population, but which were either completely unknown to our grandfathers or, if known, were, on account of their cost, quite unavailable to the man with a small or moderate income. We need not discuss whether changes in occupation are as frequent to-day as they used to be. The important point is that equilibrium is now impossible unless more extensive adaptations are made than those to which we have become accustomed in the past.

(ii) *The Difficulties of Transfer*

Failure to transfer from an old to a new industry is often the result not merely of unwillingness to face risks, nor of the desire to protect oneself against loss, but also of sheer inability to undertake the new types of work which are likely to be in demand. It is good for most of us if food is produced more easily, but it is not very cheering for the agricultural labourer who is displaced by improved methods to be told that he should enquire what else we want beside food, and then set about providing us with what we want. Perhaps we want more cinemas, or more poetry, or more motor-cars, but the displaced farm labourer cannot always easily convert himself into a movie star or a poet, or even a motor mechanic. Fundamentally the same difficulty arises when it is not merely a question of adapting people who have already chosen an occupation, but of redirecting the stream of labour which is still unspecialised. However much material progress may call for increased supplies of services of certain kinds, it will be impossible to meet the demand if an adequate proportion of the aggregate labour supply is not provided with the training and education which are needed for the performance of the necessary types of work. The connection between education and material progress has already been discussed, and here we need merely add that higher educational standards should also make us more adaptable to changes in the structure of production.

The difficulties of transfer are undoubtedly fundamental, but before examining in more detail the circumstances which are likely either to intensify or mitigate them, and the methods which might be used to meet the natural fears of loss for individuals, two circumstances should be kept in mind by anyone who is disposed to regard the difficulties as insuperable.

Especially if the appropriate rate of change is slow, the necessary adjustments may be carried through without any individual changing his work at all. If the demand for coal-miners falls off gradually, the situation will be adequately met by the sons of coal-miners seeking some employment other than that of their fathers. The problem, then, is merely one of diverting the streams of new labour and new capital which are constantly coming forward, so that they flow into channels different from those which they have entered in the past. At no time have we to deal with a static labour distribution. The volume of labour in each industry is constantly being diminished as a result of death or retirement, and increased as new workers leave school, and the necessary adjustments can be made by slowing down the rate of entry of labour into certain industries and speeding up the rate of entry into others.[1] The same point has even greater importance in relation to capital. It can seldom happen that a worker has become so highly specialised as to be completely useless in any but his own specialised field; but in many cases the literal transfer of capital, and especially of fixed capital, from one industry to another is quite impossible. If technical improvements make certain types of machine superfluous, it will often be impossible to convert such machines to any other use.

[1] Cf. Pigou, *Theory of Unemployment*, pp. 284-6.

The adaptations that are called for must therefore be made by a slackening of the flow of capital into certain older industries and an acceleration of its flow into new industries.

Further, while it is sometimes convenient to visualise the kind of change which material progress demands in the form of an individual transferring from coal-mining or wheat-farming to art or music or literature or the organisation of holiday tours, or the manufacture of high-grade furniture, it should always be remembered that a picture of this kind telescopes into one single transfer what in real life is likely to be a lengthy series of changes affecting many individuals. It would often be literally impossible for a miner to turn into a musician or a poet, but if it is made easy for some other person, perhaps a new entrant into the labour market who has a natural aptitude for these things, to enter a "tertiary" occupation, another vacancy is then created further down the scale which, after perhaps many removes, could quite easily be filled by the superfluous coal-miner. Transfers might be, and in fact often are, effected by a sort of totem dance in which a large number of people move together in the appropriate direction, each one taking the place of the man next to him. This sort of thing often happens inside a single firm when, following upon a vacancy in one of the higher executive posts, there is a series of promotions ending in the addition of a new member to the staff. Considerations of this sort make the transfers which progress demands much more manageable than they appear to be when first presented in a form the very simplicity of which may seem to render impossible a solution of the problem.

We sometimes talk as if a change of occupation were

inevitably or invariably a tragic thing. Of course it is
not something to be undertaken lightly, nor can we
cheerfully assume that it will seldom involve a decline
in the economic status of the transferred worker.
Neither, however, should we assume that a change of
occupation is in itself an evil. In every community to-
day there are thousands of people who have already
changed their occupation, and some of them more than
once, with great advantage both to themselves and to
everyone else. It is dangerous indeed to take it for
granted light-heartedly that the transfers can safely be
left to take care of themselves. But the problems which
arise are not to be solved by denying that such transfers are necessary, nor by acting as if they were undesirable.

(iii) *Proposals for avoiding the Necessity for Transfers*

(*a*) INCREASED LEISURE.—There are also two other
important side issues which should be disposed of here,
raised by the suggestions that the necessity for transfer
might be avoided, on the one hand, by shorter working
hours, or on the other by a more equal distribution of
income. The first suggestion means that, instead of
cashing scientific advance in the form of more material
wealth, we should take it out in more leisure. Sometimes it is thought that leisure should be compulsorily
thrust upon people who have passed a certain age, and
by pensions or otherwise are then induced to retire.
It is now widely admitted that there is a strong case
on other grounds for some system of compulsory retirement, but to suppose that the pensioning-off of displaced workers has any direct relevance either to fundamental solutions of the unemployment problem or to

the problem of transferring productive resources is merely another expression of pure defeatism. In effect, the rest of the community would refuse to take advantage of increased productivity and displaced workers would be compelled, whether they liked it or not, to take out the whole of their share of material progress in increased leisure.

As a device for easing the transitional difficulties when rapid technical advance demands a rapid reallocation of the labour force there is indeed something to be said for this policy as well as for the prolongation of the school period at the beginning of working life. In practice, even when the utmost care is exercised, difficulties are always likely to occur which will delay the immediate re-establishment in industry of displaced workers, and the chances of rapid absorption in the correct positions are likely to be increased if people already employed are not in the habit of remaining at work until the end of their life. Each individual retirement means a general shifting of jobs throughout the whole industry, which facilitates the re-employment of displaced men. It should, however, be clearly understood that this does not go to the root of the matter. It is at best a superficial palliative, though not necessarily to be despised on that account. Similarly, a raising of the school age should temporarily withdraw from the demoralising experience of looking for a job and not knowing where it was to be found many of those who are least able to bear it, and should also afford better opportunities for identifying and selecting the employment openings which are likely to be most advantageous. But strong as is the general case for a better educational service, it is a mistake to exaggerate its efficacy as a direct means for diminishing unemployment. If anything, it increases rather than diminishes the necessity for the transfers which we have been discussing, because it is likely to accelerate the general rate of material progress by improving the quality of work. Any relief which a prolongation of the school period gave in handling transfer problems would merely mean a temporary postponement, changes in the relative importance of different fields of employment being equally necessary whatever the statutory school age might be.

The proposal for a shorter working day, or shorter working week, has been more seriously discussed.[1] It is widely believed to have a fundamental bearing upon our problem, and deserves careful attention on many grounds. We may quite reasonably prefer to take out some of the fruits of progress in increased leisure by working a shorter day, or by taking longer and more frequent holidays or by avoiding excessive overtime.[2] Historically this trend has always been associated with industrial progress and the change has often had to be forced on reluctant industrialists;[3] but advantageous as a continuance of this trend might be on general social grounds, it would not diminish the necessity for transfers. It would merely change their form.

It is argued that because science makes it possible to produce goods, say in four-fifths of the time required in the past, working hours should be reduced by one-fifth. It is not an adequate answer to this to say that it means sacrificing all the material advantages of eco-

---

[1] Cf. "Hours of Work and Unemployment", C. A. Macartney (League of Nations Union).

[2] In some industries the development of mechanical aids has already diminished the importance of overtime. It is said that certain clerical employments have been especially affected by this trend.

[3] Cf. J. R. Hicks, *Theory of Wages*, pp. 103-10.

nomic progress; if people prefer to do this, that is their own affair, though on the whole it seems more reasonable to maintain that our average standards of productivity are not yet high enough to entitle us to call a halt. The more important point is that, even if working hours are reduced, transfers and adjustments must still be made.

The fundamental reason for this is that in the nature of things the saving of time which new inventions make possible must be very uneven. In some types of production the saving may be as much as 90 per cent, but in others the nature of the work performed makes it practically impossible to save any time at all. Transfers could be avoided by an all-round reduction of the working day, only if the working day in each industry were reduced in exact proportion to the saving in time which new inventions had there made possible or more accurately, in proportion to the time saved when due account is taken of the extent to which a lower price would stimulate demand, and this would obviously be both impracticable and unfair.

Let us examine an imaginary case, the figures in which have been selected to facilitate simple calculations. Suppose that there are only three industries, A, B and C, each employing 350,000 people, all of whom work eight hours per day. An invention in A then makes it possible to reduce the working time in that industry by three-eighths. If it were decided to realise all the advantages of this invention in greater leisure, the working day in A could be reduced to five hours. Why, however, should those who happened to be working in A receive the whole of the benefit? The case for a general reduction of hours, and not a reduction confined only to A, would, quite properly, be regarded as much more convincing. In the circumstances postulated, the same aggregate volume of production could be maintained in a seven-hour day if there were 250,000 workers in A and 400,000 in each of B and C. This would clearly necessitate the transfer from A to B and C of 100,000 workers, a number possibly greater than the number which would have to change if a general increase of production had been preferred to greater leisure. In that case there would certainly have been some expansion of demand for the cheapened products of A, and therefore less necessity for the transfer of workers from A. The main advantage of the leisure solution from the standpoint of transfers appears to be that it removes the necessity for discovering new industries. But if the increased leisure was to be well distributed over the whole of industry, many individuals would still have to seek types of employment which for them were new, and the difficulties which they would experience in so doing would not be much less than if the community decided in favour of taking the risks involved in experimenting with new types of work.

In practice there always must be some industries where the saving of time associated with new inventions could never be large. Where personal attention or manual work is essential, this is certainly so, and the growth of the numbers employed in distributive trades is a clear illustration. There are some important groups of workers for whom it is quite impossible greatly to increase physical productivity per head. The prospects of maintaining volume of production with a reduced aggregate working time are obviously very different in motor-car production and in hairdressing or in furniture production and in writing books. Whatever the advantages of a reduction in hours of work, it offers no adequate solution of the problem of adaptation in a progressive economy.[1]

(b) REDISTRIBUTION OF INCOME.—Turning now to the effects of a more equal income distribution, let us recall the conclusion already suggested that in a progressive economy it is desirable to slacken the rate of growth to which we have been accustomed in agricultural production and in the production of raw materials which are necessary to supply the basic needs of a civilised society, and to turn instead to the production of other things. To many people this conclusion seems highly paradoxical in face of the fact that throughout the world there are still large numbers of people who are unable to command adequate supplies of the basic necessities of life. The necessity for the transfers, of which we have been speaking, might be avoided or postponed, they think, by taking suitable steps for the redistribution of the world's income; instead of diminishing either absolutely or relatively the number of persons engaged in the production of butter, say, or milk, we should, it is argued, take steps to increase the incomes of people in various parts of the world who at present are unable to buy as much of these things as they would like.

Quite apart from the line of argument which is here being developed, much can be said in favour of redis-

---

[1] Cf. *Economist*, June 2, 1934, p. 1178: "The real argument for reducing hours of work is that it is socially desirable; that any decisive rise in the standard of living is impossible without it. . . . Shorter hours have not been made necessary by technological progress, but they have been made possible; or rather they have been made possible without a corresponding sacrifice in average income per head. . . . An increasing amount of leisure for the workers is now becoming an economic necessity. Without it they cannot possibly consume those secondary goods and services, the production of which is likely to create more and more employment in the future."

tribution of income, either directly through transfers based on taxation and social services or indirectly by altering the foundations on which are based both the supply of different types of work and different types of capital and the demand for them. It is also important to study the probable reactions which rapid material progress is likely to have upon income distribution. A redistribution of income does not itself, however, touch the problem of the adaptations which are necessary in the face of rapid material progress. In fact a redistribution of income would bring its own transfer problems, not the same in detail as those already indicated but of very much the same character and likely to encounter very much the same resistance. Our industrial organisation at any point of time is keyed, so to speak, to some given scheme of income distribution, and people then find employment in accordance with the habits of expenditure of those who have incomes at their disposal. It may be desirable to alter this income distribution, but if it is changed the distribution of employment must be changed too, because it is highly improbable that the groups to whom income was transferred would buy the same things as the groups whose incomes had been diminished. Equilibrium would be impossible unless the people formerly engaged in producing the goods which satisfied the desires of those whose incomes are lowered could transfer to the industries which produce the goods that the people with increased incomes now want. If an invention in any industry rendered necessary, on the assumption that income distribution remained the same, a transfer of labour and capital to industry B, a simultaneous redistribution of income could make this transfer unnecessary only if income were withdrawn from the people who would otherwise have purchased the products of B, and given to a section who would then purchase more of the products of A. The practical difficulties of ensuring that any redistribution would have this effect are clearly insuperable.

A redistribution of income would nevertheless probably have a slight retarding effect on the rate at which it was desirable to transfer resources from primary to other types of production. It is absurd to preach the hygienic value of large milk consumption when considerable sections of the population lack adequate means to purchase the supplies of milk which reasonable health standards demand. But such considerations as this do little to counterbalance the effects of the more fundamental trend which the advance of science has created. The world as a whole is not suffering from a shortage of food, and on the whole it is desirable to slow down the rate at which resources are devoted to its production. Where famines occur to-day they are more closely connected with transport deficiencies than with food deficiencies.

People who are anxious to avoid the social and economic evils associated with gross income inequalities are sometimes a little impatient when the close association between increasing wealth and changes in the character of production is emphasised, because they think that this means shirking more fundamental issues. Such emphasis, however, by no means involves ignoring these evils, which are certainly real and of first-rate importance. A clear understanding of them, however, is unlikely unless the two issues are considered separately. There is indeed, as has already been hinted, an important and intimate connection between the adaptations which material progress demands and the

reshaping of the distribution pyramid which an ac-
celerated flow of labour into occupations at present
enjoying quasi-monopolistic privileges would tend to
cause, but this is not a case of using income redistribution to avoid the necessity for transfers. On the contrary it is the transfers themselves which cause the
redistribution.

In considering the adjustments in production which
material progress demands, we must take the income
distribution at any moment as given. The adjustments
themselves will probably modify the existing distribution, and it may be advisable on other grounds to introduce further radical modifications, but it is of no
use organising production on the basis of a redistribution of income which has not yet occurred.

(iv) *Technological Unemployment*

The nature of the adaptations which material progress demands and of the processes whereby the adaptations must be carried out will be further elucidated by
a discussion of the problem of "technological" unemployment to which so much attention has recently been
paid.[1] The history of the nineteenth century is indeed
the most effective answer to those who believe that
machines, improvements in technique, are a cause of
chronic and permanent unemployment, but it is important that we should see clearly how such chronic
unemployment has in fact been avoided. The defenders
of machines have sometimes pointed to the new employment which the construction of the machines themselves calls for and the possibility of an expanding de-

---

[1] Cf. T. E. Gregory, "Rationalisation and Technical Unemployment",
Economic Journal, December 1930.

mand under the influence of lower cost and lower prices. But the instinct of the critic of machinery has been sound in regarding these defences as fundamentally incomplete. Even when full allowances are made for the new employment provided in making machines or in meeting an extended demand, labour displaced by technical improvements cannot be completely reabsorbed unless there are opportunities for transfer to other fields of employment. Ultimately the question whether technical improvements create permanent unemployment can be answered only by deciding whether the problem of transferring or diverting the stream of labour and other productive resources from old industries to new or relatively new industries is soluble or not, and we cannot decide this unless we understand the circumstances in which a demand for the products of these new industries is likely to arise.

The attempt has frequently been made to solve this problem in terms of the transfer of purchasing power. This line of approach can, however, be shown to be unsatisfactory. In a competitive industry, improvements in productive technique will tend to be reflected in lower prices, and lower prices will, without doubt, stimulate an extension of demand. The volume of employment in the industry affected will remain exactly the same, however, only in the unlikely event of the lower price inducing consumers as a whole to spend exactly the same total amount of money as before on the article whose price has fallen. As shown in a previous chapter, this will occur if the elasticity of demand is equal to unity. Moreover, if this does happen, there are likely at the same time to be some changes in the ratios between the expenditures of money allotted by consumers to the purchase of various other things, and these changes will then call for some redistribution of labour and capital elsewhere. Even if a reduced price for motor-cars or radio-sets stimulates such a demand for these things that exactly the same amount of money is spent upon them as before, the amounts spent by individual purchasers are certain to vary. Some of them will cut down their expenditure in other directions in order to buy motor-cars or radio-sets, while others, finding it possible to get these things more cheaply than they had anticipated, will have more to spend on other things. The demand for some products, and therefore for some kinds of labour, will shrink, and the demand for other kinds will expand, and to maintain equilibrium some transference of labour and capital will be necessary. The necessity for transfer will not be urgent if the industries, the products of which are in increased demand, have been working at less than full capacity. It will then be sufficient to re-employ the resources of labour and capital which have been idle. This qualification, however, is not of fundamental importance, and while it should be borne in mind, it is not necessary continually to repeat it. In any event, there is also likely to arise a necessity for some shifts of labour inside the industries affected by technical improvements, as some processes will be more important, others less important than in the past.

The more important and much more common case arises, however, where the total expenditure on the commodity whose price has fallen either falls below or exceeds the previous total, where the elasticity of demand is either less than or greater than unity.

If the total expenditure increases, it becomes necessary to divert labour and capital into the industry affected by the technical improvement, though if the prospect of getting cheaper goods stimulates to greater activity producers in other industries, who wish to increase their incomes with a view to increasing their purchases, the redistribution of labour and capital which is necessary may be more complicated. The diversion of labour and capital into industries where technical improvements are taking place will not as a rule be very difficult, but the more common situation, such as is certain to arise sooner or later in connection with every commodity which is continuously subject to technical improvement, is one in which aggregate expenditure on the cheaper commodity diminishes. In this case productive capacity will be more than sufficient to turn out the quantity of output demanded, and both capital equipment and labour will be over-supplied. In these circumstances very grave problems of reorganisation await solution. The excess capital and labour must be diverted into other industries, and if the demand for the products of other industries already in existence is unlikely to expand much, it will be necessary to discover new industries. The disappearance of technological unemployment depends upon the rapid discovery and exploitation of these new industries.[1] To explain how these diversions of labour and capital actually occur we must go beyond the approach in terms of purchasing power which has often been thought adequate. It has sometimes been said that, if prices fall as a result of technical improvements and demand

[1] Cf. Cannan, *Economic Journal*, March 1930, p. 50: "The true remedy for long-term unemployment always applied throughout history, and always effective, is redistribution of labour-force between the different occupations".

is inelastic, "the saving in purchasing power to the consumer due to the fall in prices must in fact be used for the satisfaction of other needs or else invested in fresh means of production. In both cases it represents an additional demand for labour. Similarly the extra profits which may accrue to producers through technical progress must be used by them in one or other of these ways. These supplementary profits, together with the consumers' savings, necessarily represent a total of purchasing power equal to the wages lost by the displaced workers. This purchasing power will therefore be used to provide employment for the workers displaced by technical progress." [1] This simple discussion of the problem is, however, quite unsatisfactory. There is no justification for the statement that the increased profits of producers and the savings made by consumers will be used to provide employment for workers displaced by technical progress. There is no *a priori* reason why they should have this effect. For " the increased purchasing power left in the hands of purchasers of A owing to its fall in price will be offset by the loss in earnings of the producers of A".[2] One man's gain is cancelled by another's loss, and therefore there is no net increase of purchasing power in general. Hence, if we think merely in terms of purchasing power " there is no reason to suppose that the men thrown out will find other employment".

The purchasing power explanation is no more satisfactory in those cases where, as a result of monopoly control, prices do not fall. The monopolistic gains

---

[1] Mentor Bouniatian, "Technical Progress and Unemployment", *International Labour Review*, March 1933, pp. 330-31.

[2] Pethick Lawrence, *The Money Muddle*, pp. 65-70.

which producers then retain for themselves, it is argued, effectively fill the gap in purchasing power. But the effects of the expenditure by monopolists of their additional income is again offset by the loss of earnings of the displaced workers and there is again no net increase of purchasing power. If the monopolists put the increases of income back into their businesses, the problem of adaptation is solved where their businesses happen to be those whose expansion is demanded by material progress; but often this will lead to over-expansion of the type of which we have had numerous illustrations in recent years and the problem of absorbing displaced labour then remains unsolved. If they invest the additions to their incomes in the general capital market, the case may be different. Ultimately the increased supplies of capital should lower interest rates, and thus stimulate the development of the new types of production which are needed.[1]

In any event there can be no net increase in purchasing power until the displaced labour has again been put to work. "Labour-saving techniques redistribute purchasing power but do not tend of themselves to create additional purchasing power. The increased purchasing power of other groups is exactly offset by the decreased purchasing power of the displaced worker. What these technological developments set free is not purchasing power but productive power." There is much more in this criticism than mere precision of wording. A discussion in terms of purchasing power is apt to suggest that adaptation is automatic. But a discussion in terms of productive power makes it clear that someone must take the initiative in getting

---

[1] Cf. Alvin Hansen, *Economic Stabilization in an Unbalanced World*, ch. x.

the released productive power to work. Unquestionably the main responsibility rests with the capitalist. It is important to "discourage the hope that the problem, if left to itself, will cure itself",[1] and discussion in terms of purchasing power is objectionable because it does little to effect this desirable end.

If we have been accustomed to produce, to take obvious types, a certain quantity of wheat plus a certain number of houses, of shirts, of motor-cars and of primus stoves, and if we further assume that the quantities produced of all these things are adequate, technical improvements in any of these departments of activity will undoubtedly cause unemployment, unless we arrange for the addition of new items to our production schedule. If, in consequence of improvements in wheat-farming, we can get all the wheat which we need from the labour of a smaller number of men, some wheat-farmers will inevitably be displaced, and at least temporarily deprived of the opportunity for exercising their capacity to produce. They will also be deprived of income. But permanent unemployment of this kind is inevitable only on the hypothesis that we refuse to encourage the production of new things. Once that hypothesis is abandoned, the tendency towards chronic permanent unemployment as a result of technical improvements disappears, and we are left only with the task, difficult but not unmanageable, of organising the necessary transfers of resources and tiding over the difficulties of the transition period.

It is important that we should not underestimate the significance of these difficulties. Even those who take the most optimistic view of the immediate effects of technical improvements upon unemployment have not

[1] Clay, *Post-war Unemployment Problem*, p. vii.

indeed entirely ignored the incidental individual inconvenience and suffering which such improvements
have often caused. Bouniatian, for example, who
maintains that "however rapid it may be, technical
progress cannot give rise to unemployment or become
in any way harmful to the economic life of a country",[1]
is compelled to admit that "the workers who are displaced as the result of technical progress in one branch
of production have to seek employment in other
branches or in new industries created by new inventions. They must therefore lose some time looking for
work and may even have to adapt themselves to a new
kind of occupation."[2] Most observers would be disposed
to attach much more importance than Bouniatian
allows to the difficulties of these adaptations. Among
the numerous gaps in knowledge which make difficult
an exhaustive study of the economics of material
progress is one which must some time be filled by a
realistic study of labour transfers. As early as 1835
Babbage made a plea for statistical information on this
subject,[3] which, as Gregory puts it, "after the lapse of
a century, one is still forced to echo".[4] Reluctance to
face the necessity for transfer is naturally increased if
experience has shown that in numerous instances, even
when the transfer has been smoothly completed, many
of the displaced labourers find themselves condemned
to a life of unskilled work, with a permanently lowered
income and status.[5] The realities of the situation are

---

[1] *Loc. cit.* p. 343.   [2] Pp. 331-2.
[3] *Economy of Manufactures*, para. 407.
[4] *Gold, Unemployment and Capitalism*, p. 250.
[5] *Ibid.* p. 261. Cf. G. E. Barnett, "Chapters on Machinery and Labor",
Quarterly Journal of Economics, May, August, November, 1925, February 1926; Lubin, Brookings Institute Pamphlet Series, vol. i. No. 3,
cit. Stuart Chase, *Economy of Abundance*, p. 214.

not being squarely faced if we discuss it merely in terms of aggregate employment as there may be important changes in the character of the work which new processes of production demand. Babbage showed in one instance that the introduction of power-looms had apparently caused a considerable increase in the total employed, but "it must be admitted", he added, "that the two thousand persons thrown out of work are not exactly of the same class as those called into employment by the power-looms".[1] The maintenance of the same volume of employment is quite consistent with a large number of individual displacements in which transition difficulties are serious; it is from the accumulation of these individual cases that the resentment against the necessity for change is likely to arise. But important as all these considerations are, they in no way affect the validity of the conclusion that transfers are necessary, and that they are unlikely to occur automatically.

The futility of most of the discussions which used to rage over the possibility of absolute over-production was largely the result of the fact that it was always tacitly assumed that the response of labour and capital to changes in productive technique would be prompt. As soon as improvements in any industry rendered superfluous part of the labour and capital which was employed there it would immediately be transferred somewhere else, and on this assumption it was reasonable to argue that general over-production was impossible, because there were always some unsatisfied human wants. But this assumption is quite at variance with the facts of the twentieth century. So far from the transfers being carried through promptly, there is

[1] Para. 412.

everywhere the liveliest resistance to anything of the kind. Under these circumstances, though there may be no general over-production in the strict sense, there is something which people may be pardoned for mistaking for general over-production.[1] Technological unemployment will disappear only if the hypothesis that we want the adaptations demanded by material progress is sound. If, however, we are content with existing standards, technological unemployment may be permanent, for improved technique enables us to get all we want with the employment of fewer people, and there is nothing left for the superfluous displaced workers to do.

If any community, or the world as a whole, finds that it can produce the food, the boots or the transport facilities that it has been using more easily, and therefore more cheaply than before, the essential condition for ensuring that the improvements which have taken place shall not cause unfair suffering to certain sections of the population is the rapid transfer of some of those who were formerly engaged in producing food or boots or transport services to other industries. If the transfer does not take place, the workers who now appear to be superfluous will suffer, and the rest of the community

---

[1] Cf. H. V. Hodson, *Economics of a Changing World*, p. 126. Just as there may be over-production in a very definite and real sense of any one commodity in relation to the proportion of spending power applied to it (that is to say, the money demand for it), so in the same sense there may be relative over-production, let us say, of all primary commodities together, or even of all material commodities together. There is a constant tendency for this to happen, for as the gradual progress of invention, discovery and enterprise enlarges the real income of the community, after a certain stage of material welfare is reached the community tends to devote a larger and larger proportion of its real income to services and to the elaboration of material objects rather than to food and raw materials, which means that if the total money income is constant, less and less money is spent on raw materials.

fails to get the full benefit of the improvements which have been made, partly because some provision must be made for the maintenance of the unemployed, and partly because their failure to find work which will maintain their normal level of income means further dislocation in the demand for the products of other industries, whose prosperity therefore is also endangered.

(v) *Changes in Relative Importance of Labour and Capital*

The new types of work which material progress demands will not necessarily involve transfers of labour and transfers of capital on the same scale. Technical improvements may make necessary the transfer or diversion of x per cent of the community's labour, and y per cent of its capital, and there is no reason why in general x and y should always be equal; certain circumstances indeed suggest that the relative importance of capital as a factor of production is likely to diminish in a progressive economy.

The Böhm-Bawerkian theory of capital lays great stress on the tendency towards more and more roundabout methods of production. As capital accumulates, we can with advantage make use of elaborate capital instruments, which mean a steady increase in the number of steps which separate the beginning from the end of a process of production. Böhm-Bawerk insists, however, that the law that the more roundabout methods of production are in general, if wisely chosen, the most productive has its only basis in "the experience of practical life. Economic theory does not and cannot show *a priori* that it must be so; but the unanimous experience of all the technique of production teaches us that it is so." [1] Each detour in the process of production enables us to make use of an additional auxiliary force which indirectly helps us more efficiently to reach our desired end. As the average period of production lengthens, *i.e.* as the process of production becomes more capitalistic or roundabout, the productivity of the process is also likely to increase. Serious doubts, however, arise when the attempt is made to carry this conclusion, which is valid for particular processes of production, across to a national economy considered as a whole. According to Böhm-Bawerk, "the more capitalistic the production is, the smaller will be the proportion of the year's productive powers consumed within the year, and the greater the proportion invested in intermediate products that will come to maturity as finished goods only in future years".[2] This conclusion, however, appears to overlook the possibility that, when productive capacity has expanded beyond a certain point, consumers may change the proportions between the quantities of the various kinds of goods which they wish to purchase, and if the newer things which now become relatively more important require for their production less capital in proportion than did the old, the trend which Böhm-Bawerk postulates may be reversed. There is at least no warrant for accepting his conclusion as definitely proved. It is an empirical truth that, as we pass from the primary to the secondary stage of production, the average period of production has tended to lengthen, but as tertiary products become more important history may reveal a different trend. Böhm-Bawerk indeed definitely excludes from

---

[1] *Positive Theory of Capital*, Smart's translation, p. 20; Polack's translation, p. 24.

[2] Polack, pp. 208-9; Smart, p. 91.

consideration the possibility of changes in the objects of production. "Some new type of material goods", he says, "may well be produced fortuitously and sporadically, but essentially men in general will continue to produce the same material goods as they have produced hitherto, but by other methods of production." [1]

This hypothesis must be rejected. Böhm-Bawerk makes the same error here as Sir Henry Strakosch made, and which we have already criticised.[2] Whether increased productive capacity is due mainly, as Böhm-Bawerk suggests, to increases in capital, or, as is more probable, to increase of knowledge, new types of goods, either material or immaterial, must appear inevitably, and not merely fortuitously or sporadically, and at the same time the proportions between the quantities produced of the old types are also certain to change in important respects. In a progressive economy, increases in production cannot be symmetrical.

"It is a common notion", says Cassel,[3] "that there will be a marked subsidence in the demand for fresh capital when all possible inventions have once been made, thus extinguishing the need of capital for technical developments. This sort of thing has been said as far back as any now living person can remember, but technical progress has declined to be stopped by any forecasts of these short-sighted ignoramuses. The truth is that the further technical science advances, the wider becomes the field for new technical progress, and the greater the demand for capital." But it does not follow that the demand for capital will expand either at the same rate as or more rapidly than the demand for labour as in the past. Everything

---

[1] Polack, p. 337.   [2] Cf. *supra*, p. 25.
[3] *Skandinaviska Kreditaktiebolaget*, April 1934.

clearly depends on the character of the consumer's new demands which material progress enables us to meet.

If the production periods for the goods which are necessary to meet the less urgent needs which increasing wealth enables us to satisfy are shorter on the average than the production periods required for the satisfaction of more elemental needs, then the proportion of income which must be saved if capital equipment is to be maintained will be less for a wealthy than for a poor community. In other words, a relatively small net increase in savings may give as good a return in real income in a wealthy community as a relatively big saving would in a poor community. If saving is still practised at the rate which was appropriate to maintain the capital equipment required in the earlier stages of production, and at the same time savers show reluctance to allow their capital to enter the new types of production which are appropriate to the tertiary stage, dislocation is inevitable. There is no *a priori* reason for supposing that the relative importance of capital in the production of "tertiary" products will be the same as for the production of ordinary manufactured goods, and as the importance of "tertiary" products as compared with manufactured goods becomes relatively greater we might expect some change in the relative importance of capital for the field of production as a whole. Especially where tertiary products take the form of personal or direct services, this tendency is likely to be important. The significance of this trend for forecasting the course of interest rates will be discussed later.

CHAPTER VI

CONDITIONS DETERMINING THE INTENSITY OF
RESISTANCE TO CHANGE

WE have now discussed the character of the changes
which material progress demands (Chapters II. and III.),
the risks of loss which lead many individuals to resist
these changes and the general instability which such
resistance is likely to generate (Chapters IV. and V.).
Our next task is to examine the circumstances which
are likely to make resistance to change more or less
intense. Resistance to the changes indicated by the
workings of the price and profit mechanism has always been an important element in economic organisation, but if for any reason the resistance becomes
more determined just at the time when more numerous
and more rapid changes become necessary, an element which was formerly merely an incidental inconvenience is likely to become a disruptive force
threatening the stability of the whole structure. The
extent to which this threat is likely to be important
will obviously depend in part upon the radical character of the transfers which are necessary, and in part
upon the attitude of the individuals affected towards
the changes which are required from them. The two
types of influence cannot be separated into watertight compartments, but we may, in the first place,
conveniently distinguish between certain general
influences affecting the economy as a whole and more

specific institutional factors. The general influences will be considered first, the others being left for a later chapter. If we were discussing the extent to which the risks of technological unemployment are likely to be serious, our analysis would proceed along similar lines.

(i) The general level of wealth. Transfers, as a rule, will be less necessary in a poor community because, if the efficiency of production increased, the sensible course for a poor community would be to produce more in varying proportions of the same things as it has produced in the past. The same truth can obviously be put from the opposite point of view by saying that the necessity for transfers is likely to arise more frequently in a wealthy society, where at the same time the objections to change are likely to be more keenly felt. It might be thought that in societies where people have been able to accumulate reserves there would be less difficulty in tiding over the difficulties of a transition period. This consideration is undoubtedly important, but a high level of wealth also often means a sharper sense of the value of security and therefore makes people reluctant to change their occupations. At the present time, it is not the poorest sections of the community which are most hostile to changes which seem likely to necessitate an alteration in the character of their work. The possession of "a stake in the country" is sometimes supposed to create a lively antipathy towards political instability. Whether this is either true or desirable need not here be discussed, but it is certainly true that "a stake in the country" often makes its owner actively hostile towards anything which seems to threaten his own individual economic stability.

Probably more important, however, than the sharpened sense of the value of security is the fact that in a wealthy community the range of choice of work and of investment seems bewilderingly wide, though in practice it is much limited by the necessity for specialised qualifications. The risks associated with change are thus greatly increased, and there is therefore widespread reluctance to face them. Nor is it on account of these considerations alone that high standards of wealth make the problem of adaptation to progress increasingly difficult. They introduce another complicating factor of great importance by encouraging a much greater instability of demand.[1]

It has already been pointed out that the necessity for transferring resources arises not only from greater productive capacity but also from changes of taste or fashion. The importance of these changes has always been recognised, but the fact has not always been appreciated that their importance increases rapidly when average incomes are so high that large numbers of people have a wide margin within which they can with satisfaction to themselves vary their spending habits. Apart from the transfers of resources which they themselves directly make necessary, extensive technical improvements will also create circumstances in which transfers due to changes in fashion must also be much more extensive. Demand for "bread and butter" lines is always likely to be steady and reliable. Demand for "fancy" lines is often transitory and violently fluctuating, and as the average level of incomes rises, the relative importance of "fancy" lines steadily increases. "Demand curves", it has been said, "flicker like summer lightning across the sky and the production

[1] Cf. Loveday, *Britain and World Trade*, pp. 84-112.

schedule becomes meaningless from the inclusion of selling costs." In these circumstances it is easy for an entrepreneur, who has a thoroughly sound production technique and who accurately forecasts demand for the immediate future, to be completely ruined because at a later date the public taste changes. In an extreme case demand for his products may completely disappear. Faced with these incalculable risks it is not surprising that many entrepreneurs prefer to stick to the old tried and apparently safe lines of work and investment.

Fluctuations in taste in a wealthy and progressive society introduce risks of a new kind for which the average entrepreneur is ill-prepared. The dilemma which arises in consequence has serious and widespread social implications. If an investor enters a field which is likely to flourish for a few years and then decay on account of unpredictable changes of fashion, he is likely to be ruined. But if he refuses to enter on account of the incalculable risks involved, not only does the organisation as a whole fail to register the progress of which it is capable, but the investor himself is as likely as not to be ruined in the long run on account of the chronic instability which his excessive caution introduces into the whole economy.

All these aspects of high standards of wealth have had a growing importance in our own time which, as compared with the past, is obviously a period of substantial wealth. The risks of change and the difficulties of selecting the appropriate new fields for investment appear so great that there is a chronic tendency to pour excessive supplies of resources into the industries where these risks appear to be small, and which accordingly tend to overdevelopment.

The task of identifying the new forms of production which should be encouraged in a progressive economy, and of directing towards them the appropriate flow of labour and capital, is an essential part of the *economic* problem of production. This problem has been much confused with the *technical* problem by people who, because, as they say, "the problem of production has been solved", insist that the fundamental economic problems of to-day are problems of distribution. Technical problems of production (or many of them) have no doubt been "solved" in the sense that to-day we can easily make as many hats *or* as much butter *or* as much music *or* as many museums as we like. But the economic problem of production arises because we cannot at the same time have as many hats *and* as much butter *and* as much music *and* as many museums *and* as much of an almost infinite variety of other goods and services as we like. The technical problem of production is an engineering problem; the economic problem is the problem of deciding first how much of each thing is to be produced. It is necessary somehow to choose between the wide variety of alternative types of production which is open to us, and to allot in accordance with our choice the limited supplies of resources available for production; it becomes progressively more difficult to make the allocation with precision and without friction because with rising standards of wealth there is available for us a wider range of satisfaction. It is no paradox but a sober truth that as more and more technical problems of production are solved the economic problem of production is likely to become more difficult. Every time technical conditions change, the economic problem of production has to be solved anew.

In a poor community the economic problem is comparatively simple. The range of effective choice is narrow and it is easy to determine how our resources should be used. If we are sensible obviously we would decide to devote practically the whole of our resources to the production of absolutely essential things. But when wealth increases the range of choice becomes much wider, and the task of ensuring that resources shall be allocated in such a way that our needs shall be satisfied as nearly as possible in order of their importance becomes correspondingly complicated. The number of commodities and services concerning whose purchase consumers may reasonably change their minds from year to year, or even from month to month, becomes very large, and every time consumers change their minds producers must change their occupations. The mere fact that the range of choice of occupation is wide would perhaps in itself not be sufficient to increase the relative importance of the mistakes which would be made. This is the important point: there is in any case a tendency to biassed error in the choice either of work or of investment which checks the full realisation of the potentialities of material progress. Moreover, when the range of choice among the "tertiary" occupations becomes much wider, the importance of this tendency is correspondingly increased.

In a world where technical improvements occur almost daily, there is an increasing reluctance to discuss economic problems in terms of scarcity. But although some embarrassment may be felt if the term scarcity is used loosely, the real significance of the concept is fundamental for even the wealthiest society. Its practical importance indeed is increased rather than diminished by the growth of wealth. Scarcity can be measured only in reference to the range of uses to which any allegedly scarce commodity can be put. A simple analogy may be useful here. In the middle of winter the disposition of a small quantity of coal gives us no trouble at all. We need it directly for heating purposes, and this need is so pressing that none of the numerous alternative uses ever even comes into our minds. But in summer the disposition of a much larger quantity of coal in satisfactory fashion might create a serious problem of organisation. There might be six or eight uses to which the coal could be put and a wise decision about its allocation would depend upon a proper appreciation of their relative importance. If we put too much to the seventh or eighth purpose, coal for ordinary heating might become relatively scarce even though there may be now much more of it than there used to be. If, on the contrary, we retain too much coal for its primary use, we shall suffer the inconvenience of excessive heat, and at the same time sacrifice some useful amenity which we might have enjoyed if we had used our supplies more wisely. The problem of choosing the best uses for an abundant supply of coal in the middle of summer is similar to the problem of allocating productive resources, labour, capital or land in a wealthy society. In an important sense we might say that land actually becomes more scarce the more it is opened up and developed, because new uses will then be found for it.

A similar point arises in attempting to measure or compare efficiencies. It is always the relative and not the absolute efficiency which counts. This distinction is inportant in tariff discussions. Paradoxical and even cruel as it might seem, it does not necessarily follow that a firm which can prove that its standards of

efficiency are as high as the standards of other competing firms is on that account entitled to the maintenance of conditions which will enable it to survive.
The truth of this is seen if we consider the extreme
case where, by some miracle, productivity in every
unit was suddenly doubled. All units might still be
thoroughly efficient, but if every firm worked as hard
as before, insisting that its standards of efficiency
entitled it to do so, there would be a glut. In spite of
their efficiency, some units would, from the point of
view of the advantage of the whole community, have
to turn their attention to some other kind of work.

(ii) The speed and radical nature of the improvements in productive efficiency. Where the changes are
so slow that the diversion of labour which is required
is no more rapid than the normal wastage in the labour
supply, the problem of readjustment may disappear
entirely. It has been pointed out earlier (Chapter V.)
that it is then simply a question of seeing that the
supplies of new labour which are coming forward every
year are not allowed to flow into the old industries but
are diverted instead into new channels. No individual
is forced to change his job. Boys who formerly would
have prepared themselves to drive hansom cabs are
trained instead as chauffeurs. Temporary over-supply
of some kinds of labour may then disappear very
quickly, for where skill depends upon practical training, employers will refuse to give additional labourers
an opportunity for acquiring skill which is now over-
supplied. When, however, the normal rate of wastage
is slower than the rate at which labour must be transferred, such simple adjustments are no longer enough,
and the question arises whether the problem of adaptation will be more difficult if the attempt is made to

complete the transition rapidly or whether it is desirable to create conditions in which inevitable transfers
will be made gradually. Some individuals must inevitably seek new fields of employment. Should they
be compelled to do this at once, or should an attempt
be made to lengthen out the process? "The suffering
which arises from a quick transition is undoubtedly
more intense, but it is also much less permanent than
that which results from the slower process, and if the
competition is perceived to be perfectly hopeless, the
workman will at once set himself to learn a new
development of his art" indicates the way in which
the problem was stated in 1835[1] and the same dilemma
exists to-day.[2]

Much will depend here on the character of the
industry into which the improvements are introduced.
In some industries, the adoption of a new method tends
to be rapid, especially when the reductions in cost
associated with it seem likely to be great. In other
industries, e.g. in agriculture, improvements are adopted
much more slowly and cautiously.

It is difficult to generalise confidently about the rate
at which the technique of production is changing over
the whole field of industry. If we are to judge by the
attention devoted by some popular historian to the
mechanical inventions of the early nineteenth century,
we should conclude that that period was the Golden
Age of the industrial inventor. Some account of these
inventions is commonly given even by elementary
books, and their general social effects have been widely

[1] Babbage, *Economy of Manufactures*, cit. Gregory, *Gold, Unemployment and Capitalism*, pp. 249-50.
[2] Cf. G. E. Barnett, "Machinery and Labour", *Quarterly Journal of
Economics*, November 1925, pp. 117-20.

discussed. But it is highly probable that in the aggregate the changes in our own time have been and are likely to continue to be much more far-reaching in their effects than the changes of the nineteenth century. The mechanical inventions of that time were more dramatic, partly because they stood out in such bold relief against the background of unchanging traditional methods. To-day, on the other hand, no one invention stands out so clearly because practically everywhere new methods are being adopted. They are now so common that we are no longer dazzled by their brilliance. Agriculture, transport, building and even clerical work, have all been subjected to frequent and rapid changes in technique, and in consequence the necessary transfers of resources are on quite an unprecedented scale. It is highly significant that in spite of the immense losses and dislocation caused by the War and the continual wasteful diversion of resources after the War was over into armaments and military preparations, production per head for the world as a whole had before the depression definitely risen above the pre-War level. The improvements on which material progress depended in the past were almost fortuitous, due to the unco-ordinated work of independent researchers. To-day scientific research is highly organised, and everywhere improvements in productive technique are being pertinaciously and systematically hunted down.

Further not only has knowledge expanded rapidly, but the speed with which improvements are generally adopted by the average producer has also probably increased. In particular, the average farmer is much less cautious than his predecessor fifty years ago in trying out the improved methods of work which science is

continually offering him,[1] and this still further acceler-
ates the rate at which it is desirable that transfers
should be made.

(iii) The extent to which the technical improvements
affect commodities which are already well supplied, and
for which therefore a lower price is not likely to stimulate much new demand. In a wealthy community, the
labour transfer problem created by scientific improvements in food production is likely to be more serious
than the problem created by the discovery of cheaper
methods of producing motor-cars. If the price falls,
people will buy more motor-cars, but they will buy
only a little more food.

In recent years, improvements in the technique of
production have affected many commodities which
were already well supplied, notably foodstuffs, and for
which it would therefore be unreasonable to expect
much extension of demand in response to lower prices.
The possibility of absorbing labour displaced in one
section of an industry in other sections of the same
industry has therefore become smaller and the transfers necessary to absorb the displaced labour have
accordingly become more radical.

(iv) The extent to which the new demands which the
growth of wealth makes it possible to satisfy are themselves elastic and not easily satiated. If the new demands are not of this kind but are quickly satisfied, it
will soon be necessary to carry through a new series of
transfers. As Dr. O. W. M. Sprague has put it with

[1] Cf. Sir John Russell, "The Conquest of the Wastes", *The Realist*,
June 1929, p. 40: "The greatest triumph of the nineteenth century in
the matter of food production was the discovery of artificial fertilisers.
It took farmers many years to believe that the 'chemical' was anything
more than a kind of black magic which would sooner or later ruin both
soil and farmer."

reference to the present depression, "We must look to the employment of capital and labour in the production of things for which there is an elastic demand, if we are to have a trade recovery. The direction in which an elastic demand will be found is in housing. Here is a direction in which it might be reasonably presumed that supply will encounter an effective demand, if the cost of producing houses and their appropriate furnishings is reduced."[1]

From the standpoint of this criterion, it has already been suggested that the difficulties of recent years have been unusually great. Many of the new demands which have developed have been volatile and transitory, and it has been impossible to rely upon a steady return for the resources allocated to their satisfaction. The increasing attention paid to advertising is an obvious expression of the feeling that it is desirable to stabilise demand. Demand based on advertising is, however, itself inherently unstable, for the advantage which the producers of any commodity hope to gain for themselves is always likely to be cancelled out by similarly effective action on the part of other producers, and their positions in the end are as unstable as they were at the beginning.

The possibility of taking deliberate action to create demands which are likely to be inelastic rather than demands which are easily satiated and therefore highly elastic and unreliable brings to the surface an important point which has been taken for granted throughout our analysis of the changes in demand associated with material progress. It is convenient to talk of the effects of growing wealth on consumption as if we could

[1] Cit. *Manchester Guardian*, February 21, 1933; cf. *Recovery and Common Sense*, chap. i.

arrange in order of importance the commodities and services which we are likely to buy. We shall first buy A, it is suggested, and then B, and afterwards C, D, E and so on in that order. But our demand for these things will of course be in part dependent on their prices. We will not invariably decide in favour of purchasing say K, before we spend anything on L. If L is sufficiently cheap, we may prefer it to K or even to H and J. If, as a result of an increase of wealth, we have a choice between purchasing more of K and more of L and the balance of advantage between the two is not very clear, it will be worth while tipping the balance in favour of L by offering it at low prices, if the demand for L is likely to be elastic and comparatively permanent. The satisfaction in real income will be no less, and the risks of instability for the whole economic structure will be diminished.

(v) The extent to which improvements occur simultaneously in several industries. If the rate of potential material progress is rapid, it is probable that technical improvements will be occurring simultaneously in several industries, and this fact causes further complications. A single invention by itself may cause little dislocation, if the road into other industries is not blocked by the occurrence of simultaneous changes there. But if a diversion of resources is demanded at the same time from several industries, the difficulties of discovering new outlets appear to be greatly increased. This also has been a factor of great importance in recent years. The road into many industries seems blocked to entrants from fields which have been disturbed by inventions, because elsewhere also similar disturbances have been taking place.

(vi) The rate at which population is growing.[1] Any given technical improvement will demand from a stationary population relatively more transfers than the same improvement would demand from an increasing population. Suppose, for example, that out of a population of one million 10 per cent, or 100,000, is engaged in food production, that the population is increasing at the rate of 10 per cent per annum, and that at some later date improvements in the methods of food production make it possible to get all the food that is needed from the labour of 9 per cent of the population instead of 10. At the end of the first year, 9 per cent of 1,100,000, that is 99,000 people, will be needed for food production. If we assume that the increased cheapness of food will not induce people to buy more of it, and that *per capita* consumption remains unchanged, only 1000 persons will have to be transferred to other types of work. The rest of the necessary adjustments could then be carried through merely by fewer people for a time entering the industries associated with food production. Even this small transfer would be avoided if there was some extension of the demand for food. On the other hand, if population was stationary while the improvement in production was being effected, the number needed for food production would fall from 100,000 to 90,000 and it would be necessary to transfer to other industries not 1000 but 10,000.

Errors in investment are also less likely to cause permanent loss when population is growing rapidly. If capital equipment of certain kinds is too liberally supplied ahead of the requirements of the immediate

---

[1] Cf. Lionel Robbins, "Advent of a Stationary Population", *Economica*, April 1929, pp. 76-8.

future, no great harm will be done if a rapid growth
of population catches up the growth of capital equipment which has temporarily got ahead of it. This fact
is often made the basis of appeals in "new" countries
for more active immigration policies, when it is feared
that the overhead costs of railways and other public
utilities, constructed by the State, threaten to be too
heavy.

While a stationary population makes necessary a
relatively larger volume of transfers, it is also likely
to affect detrimentally the psychological attitude of
the community towards such transfers. As compared
with an increasing population a stationary population
will include a relatively high proportion of old people
who will resist change because their minds are unlikely to be open to the idea that the development of
entirely new forms of work is necessary.

The importance of the slackening in the rate of
population growth has in other directions already been
widely recognised. Some retardation can be observed
almost everywhere, and in some countries population
is already or will shortly be stationary. Agriculturists
sometimes urge that growth of population should be
encouraged to provide a better market for the increased supplies of food which are coming forward,
and this view rests on a half-conscious recognition of
the fact that transfers are more difficult when the rate
of population increase is slow. From nearly every
standpoint, however, both economic and non-
economic, there is no reason to regret the decline in
population growth, and a recognition of the incidental
difficulties associated with it does not justify any
attempt to check it.

(vii) The extent to which the natural facilities, *e.g.*

raw material, etc., for new types of production are readily available close at hand to the displaced labour. If the released purchasing power which consumers have at their disposal is spent on goods or services which from their very nature must be produced in areas remote from the place where the displaced labour has been living, the practical difficulties of transfer are much increased. If people who enjoy the benefits of cheaper coal, for example, buy as a result of their savings on coal the products of tropical countries it is obviously difficult for displaced coal-miners to transfer themselves to the sources of production which must be developed to satisfy new needs. The importance of this in the twentieth century is also very great. New Zealanders might apply the purchasing power released by improvements in the production of butter and boots to the purchase of larger supplies of books from England, but it is scarcely feasible for persons who have been anticipating entry into butter or boot factories in New Zealand to transfer themselves for training to bookbinding or printing establishments in England. A superfluous miner cannot easily enter the oil industry. This factor also greatly increases the significance of the checks on migration which have also become almost world-wide. It is in any case difficult for an individual to shift to fields of employment in other countries, but nowadays even if he were willing to take the risk he frequently finds himself blocked by legal restrictions.

The importance of this point should not, however, be overstated. The products of tropical countries will have to be purchased by offering something in exchange. The whole process involves a raising of income standards for the inhabitants of tropical countries, and the displaced coal-miner may find employment in producing some of the things which the inhabitants of tropical countries will now be able to buy. Moreover, the market for many of the services which material progress should make more readily accessible is in the nature of things a purely local market. The services must be provided by people who live near the consumers of the services or else not at all, and where this is so, shifts of employment may be brought about without any extensive geographical movements of population. In work of this kind, natural resources, in the narrow sense, have much less importance than human resources.

(viii) The trend of the general level of prices and of general business conditions. Transfers are much easier if the price-level is such as to encourage the spirit of enterprise among the business community. When prices in general are falling, apart from the effects of technological improvements, the highest degree of willingness on the part of workers to transfer their services to new industries will be nullified if the downward trend of prices makes people unwilling to take the risk of providing capital for such experiments. This condition is obviously highly relevant at the present time; the influence of movements in the general level of prices is so important as to demand special attention, and the next chapter will be devoted to this subject.

The general attitude of the community towards the attractions of personal security as contrasted with the risks of change is, it has already been suggested, an all-pervading influence which does much to determine the importance of the various factors which have been mentioned. Where security is very highly valued, the

course of progress may indeed be completely blocked,
for there will then be little encouragement for that
development of knowledge which is one of the most
important causes of material progress. There have
been significant periods in history which could be
accurately described in such terms. To-day, however,
the urge towards the expansion of the field of knowledge is stronger and more effective than ever before;
at the same time the individual members of society
have a keener realisation of the value for them of
personal security and this greatly strengthens the
resistance to change. "In an increasing number of
bourgeois states, people are happy if they can 'hold
their own'. They want stabilisation. The slogan is
'Recovery', rather than 'Advance'."[1]

The importance of the increased desire for personal
security which is an outstanding feature of most
modern capitalist societies may be most readily appreciated if we examine the organisation of the capital
market from the standpoint of its effectiveness in distributing capital among the various competing types of
investment. If the desire for security becomes intense,
willingness to take risks diminishes and investors confine their attention to apparently sound investments
where risks are negligible. Long-dated bonds, debentures or preference shares become relatively more
attractive to them than ordinary shares. The infant
mortality rate of new industrial units is always high,
and cautious people prefer to limit their risks.[2] Such a

[1] Louis Fischer, *Fortnightly Review*, June 1934, p. 652.

[2] It has been calculated that in the United Kingdom issues of
debentures rose from 58 per cent of all borrowed capital in 1924 to
68 per cent in 1929; preferred capital rose likewise (according to the
statistics of companies examined by the *Economist*) from 56·6 per cent
of the common stock in 1924 to 58·4 per cent in 1929 (*Manchester
Guardian*, March 5, 1934).

trend tends to create an over-supply of capital for apparently assured types of production, an under-supply for newer or more speculative types.

The question then arises whether the capital market can adapt itself with sufficient promptness to the change in the outlook of investors. One of the important functions of an organised capital market is to ensure that the supplies of securities with varying degrees of risk attached to them, of common and preferred shares, bonds and debentures and other intermediate types, shall correspond as closely as possible to the supplies of capital offered by investors with temperaments displaying varying degrees of caution and venturesomeness. But however efficiently this task may be performed, the organisation will still be inadequate if the proportion of safe securities to aggregate securities differs widely from the proportion prescribed by a consideration of the rate at which new (and therefore presumably risky) enterprises should grow.

If the capital market is efficiently organised, we should expect to find the average return on gilt-edged securities rather less than the average return on speculative investments, the difference measuring the premium for risk which it is necessary to offer to attract capital into the more speculative fields. Equilibrium, once established, may be upset either by change in the relative importance of cautious and speculative investors or by a change in the supply made available by the capital market of gilt-edged and speculative securities. If investors on the whole become more cautious, more fearful of risks, the demand for gilt-edged securities will go up, and the average yield will go down, the widening of the margin between the returns on the two types of investment being an indication of the larger premium for risk which must be offered. Similarly, if the market offers too many gilt-edged securities, their value will diminish, and the average return from this type of investment will rise. The effects of adjustment of this kind are, however, likely to be extremely slow and uncertain. When caution is developed to an excessive extent among investors, the theoretical return on risky investments which is necessary to establish equilibrium in the capital market may be so high as to be practically impossible. The relation existing in any business unit between capital upon which interest is assured and the risks associated with which are therefore low, and capital the interest upon which is not guaranteed, is usually determined by the character of the business more than by the changing pyschology of investors. If the nature of a business is such as to demand some given ratio between capital with fixed-interest liabilities and equity capital, any trend which leads investors to prefer fixed-interest-bearing securities to a degree which does not correspond with this ratio may make it increasingly difficult to get new business ventures established on a sound foundation.

The extent to which the desire for individual security has grown in recent years may be most easily gauged from the growing popularity of fixed-interest-bearing securities, including government loans. Especially in a time of depression, the contrast between the eagerness with which government loan subscriptions are filled up and the widespread refusal to risk any money at all in industrial development is very striking. The low interest rates at which governments are then able to borrow are sometimes interpreted as showing how good is the government's credit. Actually they show rather how bad is the credit of everybody else, the low interest rate being in fact a pathological symptom arising from an abnormal refusal to take risks.

Even ardent apologists of capitalism have often encouraged investors in a policy of excessive caution. "It is always wise", says F. W. Hirst, for example, "to invest your savings in safety-first securities."[1] Unfortunately, if this advice is universally followed, it becomes more and more difficult to find any securities which are genuinely gilt-edged. The security of safety-first investments can be permanently assured only if an adequate proportion of the total flow of new savings is directed into channels where risks are high. If too many people dislike the risk of fluctuating returns on ordinary shares, and endeavour to ensure for themselves the security of fixed returns on bonds, the ultimate result is likely to be that all returns, including nominally fixed ones, become more fluctuating and uncertain, and at the same time the general average is reduced.

To put a slightly different point which, however, describes essentially the same difficulty, we may say that the rate at which it is desirable to float speculative enterprises is closely connected with the rate of material progress. When material progress is slow the number of openings for new ventures is small; when conditions arise which make rapid material progress possible, the number or importance of new ventures must increase at a corresponding rate. There is, however, no guarantee that the proportion of the community's supply of savings which is available for venturesome effort will

---

[1] *Lloyd's Bank Review*, July 1933; cf. L. Chamberlain and W. W. Hay, *Investment and Speculation*, p. 220, "It is a grave mistake for any but the wealthy to place capital in 'new' industries".

increase at the same time. If the savings of people of modest means who feel, and with good reason, that they cannot afford to take speculative risks, become increasingly important, the proportion may even tend to diminish. Some securities are gilt-edged, interest and repayment of savings being guaranteed as absolutely as anything can be, while at the other extreme are securities of the most wildly speculative character. Some investors prefer absolute safety, while others like a gamble, and in between the two extremes all sorts of combinations of safety and chances of large gains make their appeal to investors with varying temperaments. If the attractions of safety increase, while the need for speculative investment increases, some of the investments which are necessary in a rapidly progressive society may be quite unable to attract capital. To that extent progress will be blocked, and the risks of instability increased.[1]

---

[1] The importance of the maintenance of proper relations between the supplies of securities with varying degrees of risk can be further illustrated by reference to the controversy which has centred in recent years around the conclusions which were believed to flow from E. L. Smith's *Common Stocks as Long Investments*. It used to be supposed that trustees, for whom the safety of the savings invested should be a prime consideration, should eschew shares upon which the return was likely to be variable, and invest instead in high grade bonds on which fixed interest was paid. Basing his conclusions upon an elaborate statistical analysis of investments in bonds and in shares under varying conditions, Smith, however, argued that in the United States "well diversified lists of common stocks selected on simple and broad principles of diversification respond to some underlying factor which gives them a margin of advantage over high grade bonds for long term investments" (p. 68). An investor anxious to combine the advantages of regular income with capital security would in fact have done better to place all his savings in a well-diversified group of common stocks (or ordinary shares) than to rely upon the assurances of security which bonds appear to offer.

Smith's work has been subjected to a good deal of criticism (*e.g.* L. Chamberlain and W. W. Hay, *Investment and Speculation*; cf. Hartley

Withers, *The Quicksands of the City*, chs. viii., ix.) and it is not necessary here to evaluate fully either his theory or the rebuttals of his critics. His influence combined with that of other powerful forces, such as the activities of investment trusts, appeared to have reversed the trend in the United States in favour of fixed interest securities, and to have enlarged the flow of capital available for common stocks to such an extent as to drive up their value far above the level justified by reasonable dividend prospects (cf. Irving Fisher, *Booms and Depressions*, pp. 72-3). The application of Smith's theory which is of interest for our argument is that variations in the relation between the average returns on common stocks and on fixed interest securities might be accepted as a fair indication of changes in the average temperament of investors. If investors generally have too tender a regard for formal security, or if too large a proportion of the community's savings is invested according to the rules thought appropriate for cautious trustees, there is likely to be an unbalanced distribution of funds seeking investment respectively in common stocks and in high grade bonds. If we are thinking merely in terms of securities already in existence this trend will be reflected in a disproportion between the prices of the two types of security. This, however, is unimportant, as compared with its effects upon the distribution of new savings. It will in time tend to reflect itself in a disproportion between the quantities actually available of the various kinds of security. Company promoters will naturally endeavour to provide issues of a type which are likely to attract investors, and enterprises from which a high degree of risk is inseparable will find themselves either unable to raise capital or else tempted to offer bonds of an apparently secure type, the fixed interest upon which it may later be impossible to pay.

CHAPTER VII

THE effects of general movements of the price-level upon the willingness of investors to carry through the changes necessary for material progress are so important as to demand more detailed attention than the other influences mentioned in the last chapter. It has already been shown that the smooth functioning of a capitalist economy depends upon the prompt response by capitalists and labourers to the indications given by changes in relative prices and in relative profits. These changes, it is assumed, are the consequence either of changes in consumers' demand or of changes in methods of production. If, at the same time, prices are subjected to the influence of other trends which are not dependent upon changes of this kind, a chronic distortion is introduced into the relative price and profit mechanism, and it will be impossible to accept the indications which it gives as accurate.

Unfortunately there is no reason for supposing that the price movements which occur will be confined to those which might be expected as a result of changes in demand or changes in methods of production. In addition, there have in the past been important general inflationary or deflationary price movements due to purely monetary influences. Some of these general movements are closely connected with the swings of the trade cycle. Others are long-period movements, associated for example with movements in the value of gold or with paper inflation, as during and after the War. Whatever their cause, these price-changes stimulate movements in industry, in capital investment, which superficially are similar to the transfers already discussed. But such movements as are stimulated by variations in the general level of prices are likely to be inappropriate to the basic industrial facts. When prices are rising everywhere, efforts are made to expand production everywhere. All-round expansion of production is certainly not obviously undesirable, but a rise in the general price-level makes it difficult to discriminate between industries where rapid expansion is needed and industries where little or no expansion is required. It is probable too that capital equipment will be constructed on an elaborate scale, demanding a more abundant flow of circulating capital to keep it going than current savings will make available. The sort of expansion which a general inflationary price movement is likely to encourage will therefore inevitably tend to be unbalanced and must later break down. More obviously, when prices are falling everywhere, profits tend to disappear and production is everywhere contracted, a state of affairs which it is difficult in any circumstances to regard as desirable. In either case, the organisation of production is dislocated by general movements in the price-level.

The problems associated with fluctuations in the general level of prices have attracted much attention in recent years. But it is a little unfortunate that, in the minds of many people, the effects of unstable money upon income distribution have received so much notice as sometimes to exclude the effects upon the organisation of production, which in the long run are much more important. It is now well known that rising prices transfer wealth from the rentier, and to a less extent from the wage-earner, to the entrepreneur, and that falling prices reverse this tendency, and it is right that the considerations of equity raised by any attempt to control general price movements should be fully discussed. But considerations of equity are, strictly speaking, irrelevant to any attempt to interpret correctly the requirements of stability. An answer to that question is possible only if we place in the forefront of the discussion the effects of general price movements on the organisation of production.

It is obviously not possible here to discuss exhaustively either the general theoretical issues of credit policy which are involved, or the practical steps whereby the theoretical conclusions might be realised. So intimately connected, however, are the problems of general credit policy with the problems of maintaining stability in a progressive economy, that a brief survey of the types of stable price-level which might be aimed at should not be omitted. The main criterion to be applied, for the purposes of our argument, is not the transfer of wealth, but the extent to which the price-level facilitates or hampers the appropriate transfer of resources.

In earlier discussions of this subject it was commonly suggested—and the opinion is still widely held [1]—that credit policy should take as its goal stability of one of the standard index numbers, often of the wholesale price index number, and many schemes for ensuring such stability have been proposed. Except, however, as an indication that the grosser forms of currency dis-

[1] Cf. Alvin Hansen, *Economic Stabilization in an Unbalanced World*, p. 303.

order are being avoided, stability in the wholesale price index cannot be accepted as proof that currency policy is sound. From the standpoint of the consumer, it is clearly a good thing if the prices of the goods which he consumes fall in consequence of greater efficiency; in fact, if they do not fall, the consumer gets no benefit from increased productive efficiency and no purchasing power is released which he could use to satisfy new needs and to stimulate the development of new types of work. Nor, if they are the result of greater efficiency in production, do falling prices impose any serious handicap upon the producer. In these circumstances falling prices are offset by falling costs, and in some cases the position of the producer is made still easier by expansion of demand for his output. But falling prices, due to greater efficiency, will certainly appear to handicap producers if, when faced with an inelastic demand, they continue to expand their output. The shrinkage of profits which then occurs should serve as a signal that transfer of resources is desirable, and if the transfers are made the risk of loss for producers will disappear. It is clearly undesirable that the signal should not be given, and equally undesirable, therefore, that the price-fall should be checked. The alternative view has accordingly been widely discussed that credit policy should aim not at stability of the wholesale price index but at a price index which will move in inverse ratio to movements in the productivity of industry as a whole. This point is not one of merely academic interest as is sometimes implied by people who say that "it would be better to stabilize something than to stabilize nothing".[1]

The recent history of the United States in particular

· [1] D. H. Robertson, *International Gold Problem*, p. 24.

is in part a consequence of attempting to stabilise the wrong thing, and it is perhaps the chief defect of Sir Arthur Salter's notable book *Recovery* that he has failed to appreciate the significance of this (p. 76). On the whole he says he prefers a monetary policy which when technical improvements have occurred aims "at a compensatory upward movement of all other prices so as to keep the general world price-level the same" to one which aims "at preventing any increase in the general level which results from monetary causes, so that while industry would not be subject to a deflationary influence the cost of living would tend gradually downward". Among the reasons for this preference is the fact that "if the creditor gets as many goods or services as he provided plus his agreed interest, and the consumer pays no more on the whole for what he needs, neither has any injustice to complain about". But the important point is that considerations of justice, important as they often are, give no clear or decisive guide to policy. Unless the cost of living is allowed to fall under the impact of technical improvements, misleading indications will be given to investors and the appropriate relations between the different kinds of production will be disrupted, with a consequent tendency to depression. Whether by accident or design, the United States succeeded during the period 1923 to 1929 in maintaining a wholesale price-level which, as compared with most recent periods of similar length, could fairly be described as stable. This kind of stability turned out to be illusory, for it created the same sort of stimulus to inflationary boom as would be given if conditions of production were to remain unaltered and the price-level were to be forced up. During this period in America efficiency of production was increasing, and genuine stability demanded in these circumstances that the prices of the goods which were being produced more efficiently should be allowed to fall.[1] If such goods were sufficiently numerous, an index number which included a large number of such prices would fall too. The dislocating effects of illusory wholesale price-level stability are likely to be varied, but in particular if the prices of goods which are being produced more efficiently are not allowed to fall proportionately to the improvements in production, there is no clear indication given to producers that, in view of the greater ease with which their products can be turned out, the flow of capital and labour into their industry should be checked. Without such an indication an apparent glut is therefore highly probable.[2]

[1] Against this view it is sometimes urged that inflationary effects could be avoided by diminishing the time-lag which usually retards the adjustment of wage-rates to price movements, in this case, by raising money wages at the same time as the efficiency of production increased. But even if we do not insist upon the great practical difficulties of ensuring adequate elasticity in the wage structure, this claim still leaves untouched the inflationary effects which arise from the rigidity of long-term contracts for the payment of interest.

[2] Alvin Hansen's unqualified rejection of the view that "a fall in the price-level, caused by cost-reducing improvements in technical processes, is quite consistent with the maintenance of business prosperity" (*Economic Stabilization in an Unbalanced World*, p. 286) is based in part on a misconception of the importance of this point. "It is a striking fact", he says (p. 288), "that when rapid progress is made in the reduction of costs in any given industry, the usual rule is that such an industry instead of being prosperous is seriously depressed. At first thought one would imagine that advance in technique ought to make an industry prosperous. On the contrary such changes subject the industry as a whole to serious distress. If all producers could adopt the new methods simultaneously and to equal advantage, the whole industry would prosper from technical changes. But in point of fact this is not possible. Unequal rates of progress between firms cause serious maladjustments." This argument, however, misses the main point. If technical improvements occur in an industry turning out goods the demand for which is inelastic, it is desirable that the flow of resources into that industry should be checked and diverted into other channels

The effective choice before us is not between stabilising something and stabilising nothing. If we attempt to stabilise the wrong thing, we must end by stabilising nothing. As Robertson puts it, "if the business man's psychology jibs at swallowing the moderate price falls dictated by increasing productivity, he renders himself more and not less liable to suffer the catastrophic price falls due to industrial dislocation and crisis" [1]

Even if we accept unreservedly the conclusions of this argument from a long-run point of view, it is possible to argue, as many have done, that from time to time the price-level should be forced up a little, independently of changes in the general standard of production efficiency, with a view to encouraging the sentiment in favour of speculative ventures, which otherwise are likely to be frowned upon. This view is important when we discuss not only the nature of the transfers of labour and capital which material progress demands, but also the methods whereby the transfers might be facilitated. The point has already been stressed that technical improvements by them-

and this fact is not affected in the slightest degree by unequal rates of progress between firms. If every firm improved its technique at the same rate, the risks of over-supplying the market would be increased instead of diminished and the necessity for warning investors against maintaining the flow of capital at the old rate would be just as urgent. There is indeed no valid occasion for surprise when technical advances depress an industry the demand for whose products is inelastic. As Ricardo pointed out long ago, "great improvements in any branch of production are in their first effects injurious to the class who are engaged in that branch" (notes on Malthus' *Principles of Political Economy,* p. 51, cit. *Economic Journal,* June 1929, p. 213). Technical improvements are almost certain to cause relative over-production, unless there is a prompt transfer of resources to other industries. A stable wholesale price-level is undesirable because it makes it more difficult to recognise the necessity for such transfers.

[1] *Loc. cit.* p. 45.

selves cause no net increase in purchasing power.[1] It is productive power which is set free by technical advance, and for which therefore some new outlet must be sought. To give the entrepreneur the necessary incentive to carry the transfer through, Pethick Lawrence thought that the fall in the price-level which technical improvements would tend to encourage should be held in check.[2] Similarly, Robertson thought that "the trouble about a period of increasing productivity is that the desire to spend, not only on particular things, but on things in general, is constantly becoming temporarily saturated, so that people let balances lie idle".[3] They would tend to "hoard" their savings, holding for a time a larger proportion of their resources in liquid form. This would tend to lower the price-level further and in the depression thus created the difficulties of absorbing displaced labour would be much increased. The suggestion has therefore been made that it is necessary, so to speak, to give a jolt to business men, when the development of new industries becomes desirable, by offering them favourable credit terms which means a slight process of inflation and a slight raising of the price-level. If this conclusion is sound, then it would follow that *steady* economic progress is impossible because inflationary movements, however slight, must later produce their own reaction with a consequent temporary lack of employment for some of the factors of production.

Weighty authorities can be quoted in support of this view, but it is dangerous to push it too far. The easy money conditions which encourage speculative activi-

---

[1] *Supra*, pp. 132-3.   [2] *The Money Muddle*, pp. 65-70.
[3] *International Gold Problem*, pp. 22-3.

ties will also encourage producers who ought to change their field of activity to stay where they are, so that even from the point of view of diminishing the difficulties of transition, it is doubtful if the case for a little inflation from time to time is as strong as is often supposed. And further, the expansion of credit which might be thought necessary to counteract temporary hoarding need not necessarily be inflationary in the proper sense of that word at all. It would be merely action designed to prevent the superposition upon the effects of cost reductions of a genuinely deflationary downward movement of prices.

Whatever importance we may care to attach to mild doses of inflation as a solvent of the hesitations of cautious business men, the validity of the argument in favour of a long-period downward trend in prices, if productive efficiency is increasing, is not affected. The inflationary movement, if it is to be admitted at all, is merely a temporary interruption of a general trend which should be steadily downwards.

The general idea of the price-level movement in inverse proportion to movements in productivity is not difficult to grasp. Nevertheless it is clear that any attempt to measure exactly movements of this kind would be beset with quite unusual difficulties. Three important attempts have been made to put the idea into concrete form. First, it has been suggested that the desired end would be achieved if we were to stabilise money incomes, and in particular the value of money measured in terms of the command which it gives us over human labour. An increase in efficiency means that each unit of labour is able to produce more. If any money income X will produce at a given moment of time the product of Y units of labour, the maintenance of money incomes at X, when any or all of the Y units of labour become more efficient, will mean an increase in real income if the prices of the things more efficiently produced are allowed to fall. We might then take as our standard of stability an index number of the prices of various kinds of labour, which means an index number of earnings including wages.[1] Apart from the technical difficulties of constructing such an index number which would cover all earnings, two special points require consideration.

(a) It has been suggested that a policy of this kind would make necessary independent national currency policies. No international standard would be possible because efficiency would certainly alter at different rates in different countries.[2] There is something in this contention, but the difficulty suggested is not fundamentally a difficulty of monetary policy. It rests rather on the fact that the international mobility of labour and capital is so much hampered. If a reasonable relaxation of these checks could be assured, there would be no necessary conflict between the currency policies of different countries which were based on variations in the increase of efficiency. From the standpoint of productivity, the world must, in spite of vigorous efforts to the contrary, be regarded as a unit. Some of the transfers necessary for the maintenance of stability are international transfers and existing checks on international mobility are among the most important causes of chronic instability. In any event, "under no system of monetary policy can things be very pleasant for a country which finds the productivity of other

[1] Cf. J. M. Keynes, *Treatise on Money*, vol. i. pp. 63, 168-70.
[2] Cf. R. F. Harrod, *International Gold Problem*, p. 29.

countries in competitive goods increasing faster than its own".[1]

(b) Any policy which aims at the maintenance of stable money incomes raises the question what exactly can this mean if *relative* money incomes change, if the differences between different income grades alter as a result of variations in the supply and demand of different types of labour. Such variations are likely to occur independently of material progress, and material progress is itself likely to cause other and more important variations. As we have seen, these changes in relative money incomes need occasion no concern. But it is important to insist that, just as stability of a price index number is quite consistent with wide variations in particular prices, so stability of the general level of money earnings is perfectly consistent with radical changes in the ratios between the prices paid for various kinds of work. This point further increases the difficulty of accepting an ordinary wage index number as a satisfactory substitute for a measurement of movements in money incomes in general.

The second attempt to interpret concretely the downward price movement which increased efficiency calls for takes as its starting-point the fact that the channel through which the disturbing flow of inflationary and deflationary influences works is profit. When profits are super-normal, there is ill-balanced expansion of industry. When profits are sub-normal, there is wasteful contraction of industry. We might avoid both the ill-balanced expansion and the wasteful contraction if we could ensure the maintenance of profits in general at a "normal" level. Instead of

[1] D. H. Robertson, *loc. cit.* p. 46.

taking as our objective anything directly measurable in terms of prices, we might achieve the ultimate object in view by aiming at stability of profits. Such a suggestion raises all the difficulties involved in formulating an agreed theory of profits. Instead of talking about "normal" or stable profits, Keynes talks about zero profits, meaning what is left over after normal costs, the remuneration of management, have been met, and it is by no means easy to determine what normal remuneration of management should be. So far there have been next to no attempts at the construction directly of an index number of profits, but with an adequate information service it should not be impossible, after sufficient experience had been gained, to identify with reasonable accuracy a condition of "normal" profits, and after such a starting-point has been fixed, a good banking system which took the necessary steps for keeping in touch with business developments in general could ascertain with a high degree of accuracy when profits were tending to move either above or below normal.

The difficulty of measuring profit fluctuations, even with the most highly efficient banking system and information service, is sufficiently apparent, but an indirect indication of at least the anticipations of profit which guide the activities of business men is given by the movement of security prices. Hence it has been argued that the movement of such prices is in practice likely to be the best guide for central banking policy which is aiming at stability. Actually considerable progress has been made in the construction in many countries of index numbers suitable for this purpose. The suggestion that security price index numbers should be used in this way has also been developed from quite a different theoretical standpoint, based upon the neo-Böhm-Bawerkian theory of capital.[1]

It is not necessary here to pursue further the discussion of these important subjects. Credit theorists should, however, be constantly reminded of the necessity for keeping steadily in mind the type of transfer which a progressive economy is always needing; a sound policy must always be moulded with this end in view. An expansion of credit which encourages such transfers may perhaps be defended, but there is nothing at all to be said for an expansion which encourages people to stay where they are when they ought to move away from their customary fields of work. Many of the efforts to expand credit in recent years have been disappointing just because the necessity for transfer was overlooked. There was a great deal to be said in countries like Australia and New Zealand, for example, for a high exchange policy which provided a temporary breathing-space within which more fundamental readjustments, for example, the relative contraction of wheat and dairy-farming, and the corresponding expansion of other, newer forms of investment, could be made. Instead, policies of mild inflation have been frequently combined with deliberate efforts to stimulate further increase of production in precisely those fields where prices have been most depressed, and where therefore, according to the rules both of capitalist economy and of common sense, the rate of expansion should be

[1] F. Machlup, *Börsenkredit, Industriekredit und Kapitalbildung*, pp. 216-18: "Gold reserves and the state of the foreign exchanges must be ineffective as indices for credit and business policy if foreign countries are practising a parallel policy of inflation; the price-level will conceal inflation, if increased production paralyses credit expansion in its effects upon prices; in such a situation, the level of security prices must be a sure indicator of credit inflation." Cf. Robbins, *The Great Depression*, pp. 171-2.

slowed down. This failure to make any radical examination of our productive organisation is in large measure responsible for the new difficulties which in recent years have so much astonished people who believed that we were already well on the road to recovery. If disproportion between older and newer types of work was responsible for the dislocations which culminated in the depression, the depression could not be lifted unless such readjustments were made; to the extent to which the relief afforded by high exchange distracted attention from this fundamental necessity the effects of the high exchange policy were evil. The field within which credit policy may work with advantage is not unimportant, but even the wisest general credit policy can do nothing to remedy the evils created by chronic insistence upon pouring more capital and more labour into industries which are already over-supplied.

This discussion also enables us to offer an adequate answer to the purchasing-power puzzle which for many people prevents a ready acceptance of our general argument in favour of the more rapid expansion of "tertiary" industries. What is the use, it is asked, of producing more luxuries if we lack the purchasing power wherewith to buy them? One answer to this question has already been given. It is true that the introduction of a technical improvement does not by itself generate any additional purchasing power. Consumers (or monopolists) have more to spend, but there is an equivalent reduction in the purchasing power of displaced labourers and of capitalists who find their dividends shrinking. The volume of purchasing power will, however, be maintained as soon as productive resources are transferred to new fields. The transfer creates the new goods and services which the march of progress demands, and

at the same time the production of new goods and
services keeps up the volume of purchasing power.
From the standpoint of the individual income-receiver,
the situation presents itself in a slightly different form.
Even if his money income remains the same, a reduction in the prices of goods which are more efficiently
produced will leave him with sufficient purchasing
power released to buy some of the new goods and
services. If resources are transferred without delay, and
prices are allowed to fall in harmony with movements
in cost of production, alarms about deficiencies of purchasing power are quite unnecessary.

CHAPTER VIII

THE steady diversion of labour and capital away from industries which are well established into newer and relatively more risky enterprises is, as we have shown, an essential condition for the maintenance of stability in any economy where the objective conditions exist which make material progress possible. In particular it is an essential condition for obedience to the rule of a capitalist economy which requires transfer of resources from less remunerative to more remunerative fields. We have already examined some of the general influences affecting either the economy as a whole, or the character of the technical improvements which are made, which prevent or unduly delay these necessary transfers.

In addition, however, there are certain other influences, which may roughly be described as institutional, which further complicate the situation and increase the difficulties in the way of making such transfers. In the first place we have the difficulty in practice of identifying those industries whose rapid expansion is demanded by the exigencies of material progress. When in times like the present, it is pointed out that a greater willingness to take risks in expanding investment in relatively untried fields is essential if there is to be satisfactory economic recovery, the practical man is inclined to ask with some impatience for more specific directions. He finds a plea for more investment in general unconvincing, and wants to know in what particular direction it is his duty to take new risks.

It must be admitted at the outset that circumstances are possible in which action is desirable of a kind for which the movement of relative prices and relative profits can give no guide whatever. The necessity will arise from time to time for stimulating production of an entirely new kind, and because it is entirely new, it is obviously impossible to make any reference whatever to the prices or profits of the past. In a growing economy, there will occasionally be a definite blind spot somewhere, which makes the anticipation of new wants, the nature of which is absolutely unknown, the task which the innovating entrepreneur must tackle.

But important though this may sometimes be, the much more common case will be one where it is the duty of the innovating entrepreneur to expand fields of production which hitherto have been relatively unimportant. Which field is he to select? To this question the economist can give two general answers. Starting from the hypothesis of a rising level of average real income, we can say that it is the task of the entrepreneur to organise the production of those things which people with rising real incomes will want to buy. It is not possible to predict with confidence how any particular individual will spend his income if it is increased. Sometimes we ourselves find that if we are fortunate enough to receive an increased income we spend the increase in a way quite different from that which, if we ever reflected upon such possibilities, we had pictured to ourselves beforehand. But the impossibility of predicting how individuals will spend increased income is quite consistent with a high degree of certainty about the expenditure habits of groups. On the whole, a group whose average annual income had been, say, £200, will, if the average is raised to £220, spend the additional £20 in much the same way as people do whose income is already £220, and so on right through the scale. It is in fact on some such hypothesis as this that the whole of our general analysis of production and consumption in a progressive economy has been based.

This principle, important as it is, gives us, however, only a very rough and vague guide. Making his interpretation of the rules of capitalist economy a little more definite, the economist can urge the investor to put more money into those industries where the rate of profit has tended to be above the average. Even if all industries were depressed there would be some which would be less depressed than others, and into these it is desirable that the flow of capital should be directed. The economist must confess that he has great difficulty in picking out specific industries and saying confidently, "These are the industries where more capital should be invested". This is not, however, his fault, but the fault rather of those people who imagine it to be to their interest to conceal the facts in the absence of which a satisfactory comparison of profits is impossible. The most important difficulty in the way of obeying the fundamental rule of a capitalist economy is therefore in part a statistical difficulty. All the facts about profits are presumably available somewhere, but at present we have no satisfactory means of getting at them.

Even if all the facts were available for everybody the position would not be easy. The existence of monopoly creates no real difficulty from the standpoint of identifying the fields where more investment is needed, though it is highly important as illustrating the power of the vested interests which check wise action. Where monopoly profits are unduly high, either production should be expanded or the monopolists' price policy should be controlled. In competitive industry, however, the return on capital investment in the past may be a quite misleading indicator for guiding investment in the future. High profits may be enjoyed even for considerable periods in industries into which it would be most unwise to pour further capital. There is no special virtue about the year which makes it the only suitable period in reference to which profits are to be measured, and it is necessary to take much longer views. Adequate allowance must be made for variations in risk and for the provision which it is prudent to make for losses arising from wasting assets. Some projects involving heavy capital expenditure, *e.g.* railway electrification, may be thoroughly economic even though the immediate return may be small for some time.

The fact that an industry is showing high profits may mean that it is under-developed, and therefore more capital should be introduced into it. Alternatively it may mean that the industry is likely to disappear altogether in the near future and that the risks of loss for investors are therefore so great that high returns are necessary to attract any capital at all. An important illustration of this is the risk already referred to of over-development of certain luxury industries the return on which was for a period high. Many investors in ephemeral forms of amusement in recent years have had practical experience of the difficulties in a progressive economy of maintaining the appropriate flow of capital. It is important not to be deceived by merely temporary flashes of prosperity. Similarly, if profits fall in certain industries, that may mean that risks are declining, that the industries have become well established, and that increased, rather than diminished, supplies of new capital are needed. Nominal profit rates are often meaningless from the point of view which we here have in mind, because they depend so much on nominal capital valuations. A completely satisfactory interpretation of profit in any specific instance would often entail an elaborate analysis of the whole history and especially of the financial history of the unit in question. On this account, more importance has sometimes been attached for some purposes to the rate of profit on turnover. A direct comparison of rates of profit on turnover in different industries would, however, be meaningless, because the normal rates vary so widely. Relative changes in the rate of profit on turnover might nevertheless give useful indications of changes in the relative attractiveness of different industries. The profit that is most important for our purpose is that earned on the units of capital which have just entered or are just entering each industry and this profit will be difficult to identify.

We must also distinguish between changes of profit in industries as a whole, and changes in particular units. Increasing profits in one unit would not necessarily indicate that it was desirable to expand the industry as a whole. It might merely mean that that unit should be expanded at the expense of other units in the same industry. It will often happen that even when an industry is declining as a whole it will include some prosperous, perhaps even very prosperous units, whose expansion should be encouraged.

While it is important to avoid anything which might

suggest that the rule for investment in a progressive capitalist society could in practice be applied easily or automatically, it is more important not to suggest that the barriers are insuperable. They are in fact surmounted every time a successful investment is made, and at many periods of history successful investments have been numerous. And it is even more important to insist that the most serious of the practical difficulties which arise here have their origin, not in the inherent difficulty of the material which has to be handled, but in the deeply rooted prejudice of the average business man in favour of secrecy. It may be indeed that we touch here the most fundamental contradiction which threatens the stability of the capitalist system. If the system is to function smoothly, it is necessary—and incidentally, to the interest of every member of society— that adequate information should be available to investors to enable them to direct the flow of savings into the proper channels. At the same time, however, it appears to be to the interest of each individual to prevent potential rivals from having access to that information the absence of which threatens the security of everybody. Self-interest leads every entrepreneur, anxious to protect himself against the risks of competition, to maintain an attitude the general adoption of which is no less to his detriment than it is to the detriment of all his rivals.[1]

---

[1] It should be noted that the points raised here are quite different from those involved in Pigou's analysis of divergence between marginal social net product and marginal private net product. The divergences which Pigou discusses keep the national income at an unnecessarily low level but they do not necessarily involve any instability in the economic structure. Pigou argues that the encouragement of investment in increasing returns industries by way of bounty might under some circumstances be legitimate, but the basis for this belief is not the fact that in the absence of such bounties the products of these industries

The second institutional factor to be considered as influencing the flow of capital is taxation policy. Taxation burdens are sometimes alleged to retard industrial development in general. The question whether taxation diminishes saving in the aggregate does not arise here, but the question does arise whether it is likely to distort the distribution of capital, encouraging certain types of industry out of proportion to others. Taxation is sometimes definitely designed to encourage specific types of industry. Customs duties nearly always are imposed for that purpose. Municipal rates may also be remitted from certain types of enterprise, and agriculture has frequently been favoured in this way. Any taxation of this kind may strengthen the tendency towards maldistribution of capital, unless there is reason to believe that other influences pointing in the opposite direction and tending towards under-investment require to be counteracted. There is, for example, an arguable case for special favours for agriculture, because of the handicaps imposed by its apparent unsuitability for joint-stock enterprise. The most interesting point in connection with taxation is, however, a more subtle one, that of the effect of graduated income-tax in discouraging speculative enterprise. If 5 per cent is the normal return on capital, but in a particular industry 7 per cent is necessary on account of unusual risks, graduated income-tax, it is argued, will fall with undue weight on the 2 per cent risk premium, and with steep graduation, all the payments made for bearing risks will be affected in a similar way. Hence it is claimed that investors will avoid risky

are likely to be so under-supplied relative to the products of other industries as to cause that general instability which we have been endeavouring to explain.

undertakings and prefer gilt-edged securities. "A speculative stock, if it is to attract capital, must offer a return over and above the gilt-edged rate of interest such as to provide an adequate premium for the general and specific risks of the business. Income-tax and super-tax, when heavily increased, may so cut into the rich investor's return that the premium element is no longer sufficient, on an actuarial basis, to cover the valuation of possible loss. In such circumstances, capital from the wealthy class of speculators cannot in the long run continue to be attracted. Any taxation which unduly diminishes the reward of entrepreneurs for taking pioneer risks is in that respect a source of harm to the community."[1]

The same point is raised by the question of averaging incomes over a series of years to ascertain the income on which income-tax should be assessed in any given year, and by the suggestion that business profits which are transferred direct to reserves should be exempt from taxation. It is not merely a question of equity as between different taxpayers, but, much more import-ant, a question of encouraging or discouraging activity or investment of certain kinds as compared with others. The Colwyn Committee discussed this problem from many angles, but decided that on the whole its import-ance was not very great. High graduated taxation might have, they believed, a slight deterrent effect upon enterprise but nothing that called for a reversal of policy. The majority of the Committee agreed that company reserves were "a form of saving which is of special value to the community" (p. 149), because there is less delay and economic friction before the saving becomes effective, and such capital is likely to be

[1] Report of Colwyn Committee on National Debt and Taxation, p.142.

applied "just in the place where it is required . . . at
the growing point of industry, enabling new needs and
opportunities to be met without delay as and when they
arise".[1] Income-tax, it was also agreed, was likely to
diminish this form of saving, but taking all the relevant
considerations into account, it was concluded that no
"grave damage has been done to company savings in
general". This conclusion has recently been criticised,
in part on the ground that the Committee was too
much influenced by its interpretation of the peculiar
conditions of 1924. "If we wish to bring about a new
orientation of industry adapted to the changed post-
war needs, the concerns that we must encourage and
assist are those that are expanding in new directions,
or by some other means contriving to earn profits. Our
aid must be selective, not general; a uniform stimulus
to all firms, which might be effective if we had been
in the trough of an ordinary trade depression, would
have left the orientation of industry unchanged and the
maladjustment unremedied. 'To him that hath', not
'Unto this last', must be the principle on which
stimulus must be applied."[2] Heavy taxation on company reserves, it is argued, prevents such a discriminating stimulus from being effectively applied.

These points probably have some importance, but
not so much as might be attributed to them if we made
merely an abstract analysis of the investment market.
For some persons the influence of high taxation on

[1] Alvin Hansen suggests some doubts as to whether the reinvestment
of profits by employers in their own businesses will not in fact lead to
a misdirection of capital. "The cartel form of organization is especially
guilty of blindly putting profits back in the business until capital equipment has expanded to a point where there is gross overcapacity"
(*Economic Stabilization in an Unbalanced World*, p. 169).

[2] Henry Clay, *The Financing of Industrial Enterprise*, Manchester
Statistical Society, March 9, 1932, pp. 21-2.

investment might be exactly the reverse of that suggested by the critics of steeply graduated income-tax; instead of avoiding risky enterprises because the risk premiums were taxed at a high rate, they would be prepared to take bigger risks than in the past in the hope of maintaining their income, in spite of high taxation. Real risks of investment would not change, but the investors' subjective estimates of risk might alter to a considerable degree.[1] Further it is probable that for large enterprises the point is less important than for small; losses in one department can be offset by gains elsewhere, so that although risks in each department may be considerable they tend to cancel out for the enterprise as a whole. Nevertheless when all the reasonable qualifications have been admitted, the possibility that high graduated income-tax will further encourage the tendency to allocate an undue proportion of the community's savings to apparently safe forms of investment should not be neglected when we are endeavouring to formulate a far-seeing policy of taxation. The purposes for which the proceeds from taxation are spent also have some relevance here.

Something has already been said concerning the functions of the capital market in providing adequate supplies of securities graduated according to the risk involved and sufficient to attract investors whose temperaments display varying degrees of caution. There is clearly no guarantee that the ratios between

---

[1] Cf. Mr W. H. Coates's evidence before the Colwyn Committee: "Man's comparison between disutility and utility, effort and reward is not a constant factor; it is a moving factor, and it is conditioned by the terms and circumstances in which the man lives. One judges things differently according to the circumstances which may exist, and what may be not enough to tempt a man of fifty-five, may to-day tempt a man of twenty-five strongly, and you have got every degree in between" (cit. *Economic Journal*, December 1927, p. 580 n.).

the supplies of different types of security will always be exactly right, and the organisation of the capital market must therefore be included as another institutional factor which may check the flow of capital along the channels which are demanded by material progress. In Great Britain, for example, many have argued that in recent years the organisation of the capital market has been such as to encourage an excessive flow of capital into foreign investments; investors have been deceived by the apparent security offered by Government guarantees, and have discovered later that these apparently secure investments were in fact highly speculative. Though this trend has in fact increased the supply of capital in certain speculative parts of the world economy beyond reasonable limits, it is at the same time an expression of the general desire for security.

The Macmillan Committee believed that in the English capital market a defect of another kind checked the distribution of capital along the best channels (Report, 1931, pp. 161-74). It was argued that the machinery for distributing short-term credit in England was working fairly smoothly, and that the institutions, *e.g.* accepting houses, etc., for allocating capital on a large scale, and especially for investment abroad were also fairly adequate. But "great difficulty", it was said, "is experienced by the small and medium-sized businesses in raising the capital which they may from time to time require even when the security offered is perfectly sound" (p. 173). The standpoint from which the capital market as a whole is commonly discussed is that of the waste and loss of capital which are often the consequences of the misguided choice of individual investors. This is no doubt important, but the point with which we are more concerned here is the fact that the absence of adequate machinery means that certain types of industrial organisation are starved of capital. If it happens that these types are to any considerable extent those which the trend of industry in a progressive economy makes peculiarly desirable, the inadequacy of the machinery of the capital market itself is an important factor checking the adaptations which material progress demands. "The rôle of new enterprises is to turn the flank of depression by finding new outlets for industry in which the price which the consumer can be tempted to pay by the novelty of the object offered him will cover the expenses of production. No recovery after a slump takes place without an extensive shift of industrial activity to producing new products, new varieties of old products, and for new markets",[1] and if such shifts are checked because of the difficulty of getting access to adequate supplies of capital, the depression will be indefinitely prolonged. There is little doubt that this problem is an important one in many countries other than Great Britain.

It is unfortunate that the phrase "investment trust" is often used loosely without any effort at clear definition, but the development of these institutions is another influential factor in the modern capital market, which is likely to affect the flow of capital into various channels, and incidentally may modify the effects which were discussed above of taxation upon the distribution of capital. Estimates of risk are likely to be, and should be, more conservative for small investors than for large. Reluctance to supply capital for

---

[1] Clay, *Financing of Industrial Enterprise*, p. 7.

new and risky investments and the dislocations which ill-balanced development cause will therefore tend to be greater in a community where small savings are predominant than where all investors have large supplies of capital at their disposal. The effects of the natural and wise conservatism of small investors can, however, be counteracted by the organisation of investment trusts without subjecting investors to unnecessary risks. Investment trusts are in effect instruments for ensuring that all investors may, if they wish, behave as large investors commonly do in averaging risks. If it is the small investor who tends to lag behind in exploring new types of production, the investment trust may make easier the maintenance of equilibrium. The burden of risk-bearing no longer falls so obviously and directly upon the individual investor and there is therefore less likelihood of excessive caution leading to an over-supply of capital seeking safe outlets.

It is possible that as time goes on, investment trusts will more and more actually have an important stabilising influence. At the present time their reputation is a little damaged, and like other new institutions, they are clearly liable in the earlier stages of their history to certain abuses. If they should be extensively developed and become successful, it will be interesting to speculate upon the influence which they are likely to have upon the theoretical foundations of capitalist economy. The invention of the joint stock company damaged the old *laissez-faire* philosophy by showing that efficient work remunerated by salary was possible, but the investor still maintained at least a nominal independence in deciding what enterprises should be developed. When he hands over his savings to an investment trust his independence in this field also becomes extremely shadowy.

A great deal of attention has also been given to the effects of rigid wage policy in upsetting the equilibrium of the economic structure; this is relevant to our discussion because the refusal to allow relative wage rates to change is one way of obstructing the movement of labour from industry to industry. It is unwise to deny the force of this contention altogether. There is excellent authority for supposing that rigid wage rates have been one cause of the persistence of the depression. It is not necessary here to attempt to settle the controversy which has raged over the effects of wage reductions upon purchasing power,[1] but at least, in some important instances, there is little doubt that too rigid adherence to customary wage rates has checked the appropriate transfer of labour from one set of industries to another, and in countries where unemployment insurance exists it too has no doubt been a factor strengthening this tendency, though that by no means proves that unemployment insurance is bad.

Too much, however, must not be made of this point. In the first place, it should be noted that from the standpoint of the argument which is here being developed, flexible wage rates are necessary merely as stimuli diverting labour into new fields. General wage changes, which leave the existing distribution of labour unaltered, are quite useless from this point of view. Further, wages must be interpreted in the widest possible way to include payments for all classes of work. Reference has already been made to the dislocating effects of attempts to maintain professional incomes at their customary level. Rigidity in this field

[1] Cf. E. R. Walker, *Australia in the World Depression*, pp. 168-203.

may have consequences more serious than rigidity of wages in a more popular sense of the word. And thirdly, rigidity of labour costs cannot reasonably be discussed as an influence unaffected by rigidity in other parts of the price structure. Labour is demanded jointly with all the other elements which are necessary for production. If some of the available labour is unsold, that may indicate not that the price of labour is too high, but that the price of some of the other elements which should be associated with labour is too high. On the whole interest charges tend to be much more rigid than wage costs and this fact is important in two ways. First, the rigidity of the interest burdens imposed in periods of falling prices by long-term contracts greatly diminishes the prospects of speedy recovery. And secondly, and more important from the standpoint of a re-orientation of the direction of production as a whole, the general refusal by investors to recognise that the equilibrium rate of interest has fallen leads to waste of capital, and a disinclination to invest it in investments which are thoroughly sound, but can offer only a return lower than that to which investors have become accustomed. As the part played by "tertiary" products in the economy as a whole becomes more important, the equilibrium rate of interest is likely to fall. In the production of these things capital is likely to play a relatively less important part than it did at many stages of primary and secondary production, and if, as a result of rapid material progress, the demand for "tertiary" products increases more rapidly than the demand for other things, the demand for capital relative to its supply will slacken a little, so that the rate of interest tends to fall. Investors, however, dislike the lower rate of interest which a slackening of the need for capital is likely to bring with it, and in consequence either endeavour to keep their capital uninvested until more attractive opportunities are open, or else uncritically devote their savings to enterprises where the returns seem to be high, largely because they are normally associated with a considerable risk premium. One reason why long-term money rates fell so slowly in 1929 and 1930, it has been said, was "probably that investors had for many years been used to considerably higher returns on their capital than before the War, and had come to regard this high level as natural and normal. Hence they were averse from accepting a lower yield, and preferred to keep their money on short term in expectation of some more promising future opening." [1] At the present time, a high degree of willingness to take up Government bonds is frequently combined with great activity in highly speculative but traditional fields like gold-mining, in which many new enterprises rest upon extremely shaky foundations. Investors look askance at ordinary commercial propositions which offer only a moderate return; that their shyness cannot be completely explained by nervousness about the nature of the securities offered is shown by the marked increase of activity in mining shares which are notoriously risky. In many cases the ultimate result of reluctance to invest is complete disappearance of capital, the rate of interest being thus maintained by methods not unlike those used by the people who burn coffee or wheat, or dump surplus fish back into the sea.

Finally, in forming an opinion about the desirability of checking agricultural and pastoral development in

[1] *Course and Phases of the World Depression*, pp. 225-6.

countries which by reason both of natural resources and business traditions appear to be particularly suitable for activities of that kind, it is important to pay attention to tariff policy. It has here been urged strongly that the normal course of material progress demands a relative decline in the importance of agriculture as a field for employment. The world already has more farmers than are necessary. But, it can be argued in particular countries, the apparent necessity for checking the rate of growth of primary production arises not from the essential character of material progress itself so much as from the barriers created by other groups interested in protecting themselves against the risks of change. Farming appears to be relatively unprofitable, it is argued, because of the costs imposed upon farmers by tariffs raised for the protection of manufacturers. If tariffs were reduced, farming would no longer be unprofitable, and it would be reasonable to invest more capital in it. Or in more general terms, those industries which are relatively least profitable when tariff barriers are important may improve their position if the barriers are removed. This argument undoubtedly has some validity, but it does not seriously alter the general character of our conclusions. An increased activity in primary production in Australia and New Zealand, for example, is justified only on the assumption that people in other countries are ordering their productive activities in accordance with the principle demanded by material progress. With or without tariff barriers, the general presumption is still in favour of a relative slackening in the rate of growth of agriculture.

CHAPTER IX

MAINTENANCE OF APPROPRIATE PROPORTIONS BETWEEN
CONSUMERS' GOODS AND VARIOUS TYPES OF PRO-
DUCERS' GOODS

IT has already been pointed out that we are not concerned here to offer a complete theory of the business
cycle; it is therefore unnecessary to criticise or evaluate
the other explanations which have been put forward
for this purpose. There are, however, two important
business cycle theories about which something should
be said. The transfers of resources which have been discussed so far, as relevant to the problem of organising
material progress, have been in the main transfers between industries engaged in the provision of goods for
consumers. Most of the illustrations which have been
used have suggested that the most important dislocations which we have to consider are those which affect
the distribution of productive resources between the
various groups of industries which cater for different
kinds of consumers' goods. We have on the whole
neglected the possibility of error in the distribution of
resources as between consumers' goods in general and
capital goods in general, or as between the kinds of
capital goods which are needed at successive stages of
production. Clearly this assumption may not be war-
ranted by the facts, and we should therefore examine
two theories which, though diametrically opposed, are
similar in making errors of the kind which we have so

far neglected the root cause of industrial fluctuations. An examination of these theories is especially useful, because it can be shown that our thesis throws much light upon the phenomena on which they are based.

Let us take first J. A. Hobson's theory of over-saving or under-consumption. Hobson maintains that there is a chronic tendency for capital equipment to be produced in excessive quantities, mainly in consequence of the automatic savings of wealthy people, but partly also because of conservatism in expenditure. Over-investment is constantly occurring, and the goods which are produced cannot be bought at prices which fully cover costs because the consuming power of that part of the community which has not saved to excess is inadequate. On this foundation Hobson builds up his theory of the trade cycle. The maintenance of stability depends upon the maintenance of the proper ratio between saving and spending. This ratio is constantly being upset, and as industry becomes unprofitable when consumers are unable to purchase its products, the economy suffers from recurrent depression.

The fundamental orthodox reply to Hobson[1] is that, provided the economic structure as a whole is flexible, there is no reason why equilibrium should not be maintained whatever the ratio between spending and saving may happen to be; if savings were excessive at any time, the rate of interest would fall so low as to check any undue tendency towards capital accumulation. Further, if savings are wisely invested, the new accumulations of capital will make possible a reduction of prices which prevents any deficiency of consuming power.

---

[1] Lionel Robbins, "Consumption and the Trade Cycle", *Economica*, November 1932.

The proviso that "the economic structure is flexible" is obviously of great practical importance, especially in its application to interest rates. If investors as a whole refuse to face the fact that the equilibrium interest rate is falling in a progressive economy, and insist on taking steps which are likely to keep it at the customary level, the results will be inconsistent with those suggested by the orthodox criticism of Hobson. Capital will be withheld from the newer types of production which ought to be developed, and the equilibrium of the whole economy will be upset.

If, however, we abandon the hypothesis that individual errors in investment may be ignored because in the aggregate they tend to cancel each other, and admit the importance of the forces which tend to create chronic and cumulative errors, we are able to offer for the appearance of over-saving, upon which Hobson insists, a partial explanation which cuts across the whole of this controversy. The appearance of over-saving will be given if investors are reluctant to put their savings into the new industries for which material progress calls and instead keep on pushing them into the old industries. However difficult it may be to estimate accurately the volume of saving which is desirable for any purpose, it is possible that the aggregate, however estimated, may be just right, but if there is a chronic tendency towards maldistribution of capital, towards the neglect of new industries and the paying of too much attention to the old, some savings will be wasted and the appearance of the general situation will be similar in important respects to that to which Hobson directs attention.

Hayek's theory, like Hobson's, also raises wider issues than those with which we need here to concern ourselves. For our purposes the essential part of his theory of capital is its insistence upon the necessity for maintaining the correct proportions between the various kinds of capital which are needed at successive stages of production. Capital is important because it enables us to use more roundabout and more efficient methods of production. If the supplies of capital increase, productive processes tend to lengthen, because it is then advantageous for us to interpose additional stages between the beginning of production and the sale of the product to the final consumer. After we have once created a very roundabout, highly capitalistic mode of production in any industry, a steady flow of various kinds of capital, raw material, semi-finished articles, etc., is necessary to keep the process of production going. If this flow is not forthcoming in the appropriate proportions, some of the elaborate equipment which has been constructed will have to be abandoned, and the community will have to satisfy itself with less roundabout methods of production; in the transitional period which is necessary to carry through the incidental adjustments, both capital equipment and labour will be unemployed.

This deficiency in the supply of working capital necessary to keep elaborate equipment at work would occur if the volume of saving were to decline. It would also happen if purchasers of capital goods were induced to act as if there had been additional saving, whereas in fact there had not.

Hayek maintains that credit inflation is an artificial stimulus which induces people to act as if there had been additional saving, and the effects of which cannot be permanent. Credit inflation means forced saving imposed through the medium of higher prices, which diminish the real incomes of persons with fixed or relatively fixed money incomes. The resultant stimulus which such forced saving gives to the production of elaborate capital equipment cannot be maintained indefinitely, and when it slackens off there will be an inadequate supply of saving to provide enough working capital to keep the equipment going. The equipment thus appears to be superfluous and has to be left derelict. Hayek says that "the situation would be similar to that of a people of an isolated island, if, after having partially constructed an enormous machine they found out that they had exhausted their supply of savings and available free capital before the new machine could turn out its product. They would then have no choice but to abandon temporarily the work of the new process and to devote all their labour to producing their daily food without any capital."[1] The moral follows that such forced saving is bad, because it leads to the creation of capital equipment out of proportion to the supplies of saving which are likely to be forthcoming later. It has been suggested that this theory fits certain facts of the American slump better than any other explanation.[2]

This is in some respects the exact opposite of Hobson's theory, but much the same comment can be made upon it. It is true that after a crisis there is much capital equipment left derelict in a way which seems compatible with Hayek's theory, but the fact is equally compatible with the theory that there is a chronic tendency to relative over-investment in the old-established industries. The industries which after the crisis are found to be over-developed are not necessarily

[1] *Prices and Production*, p. 84.
[2] Robbins, preface to *Prices and Production*, p. xi.

those which have extremely roundabout methods of production. It is not that the capital units are organised on the assumption that larger supplies of working capital will be available than is actually the case, but that there are too many duplicate units of the same kind. In New Zealand, for example, we had too many freezing works, and too many branch railway lines, while farming was over-capitalised in the same way. This consideration does not prove that Hayek is wrong, but it does suggest a substantial and probably important alternative. As Robbins puts it, on Hobson's view we "starve in the midst of plenty" because we seek to pluck the fruits of prosperity before they are actually ripe. It is never fair to criticise a metaphor too harshly, but this method of describing the situation certainly suggests the fundamentally erroneous view that prosperity depends on cultivating the trees we already have. On the view suggested here some of us starve because we keep on planting too many of the old familiar types of tree, the methods of cultivating the fruit of which have so improved that it is easy for supplies to become excessive.

Hayek in effect says that the existence of derelict capital is an indication that capital goods have been produced for which it has been discovered later there is no demand, because the necessary corresponding saving is not forthcoming.[1] "The Trade Cycle consists first in setting up a Rate of Investment that cannot be maintained and then in recovering painfully from the muddle into which this process has forced us." But the existence of derelict capital may equally well indicate that the wrong types of capital goods have been produced. The development of capital equipment

[1] E. F. Durbin, *Purchasing Power and Trade Depression*, pp. 143-4.

has not necessarily been pushed further than can be maintained by current habits of saving, but has instead been turned into the wrong channels.

The disharmony in capital distribution which we have here been discussing is again different from the "far-reaching economic disharmony" which many high authorities have discovered[1] in an alleged tendency to underrate future satisfactions, and therefore to fail to accumulate supplies of capital which, from a long-range point of view, should be regarded as adequate. It is doubtful indeed whether this tendency is as important as has been supposed, but even if it was the disharmony involved is not the sort of disharmony with which we have been concerned. In spite of any disharmony arising from inadequate saving, stability would still be possible at every stage. Such disharmony arises, if at all, because we sacrifice too much future satisfaction in order to make certain of present satisfactions, but this loss is quite compatible with the maintenance of stability. The disharmony with which we are concerned arises because the aggregate supply of savings, whether inadequate or not, is wrongly distributed between the competing fields of investment.

[1] Cf. Pigou, *Public Finance*, pp. 121-2.

CHAPTER X

SOME PRACTICAL SUGGESTIONS

THE general drift of our argument should now be clear. The prompt and continuous diversion of labour and capital into relatively new types of production is an essential condition for maintaining a satisfactory rate of material progress, as well as for avoiding chronic relapse into depression, or if we happen for any reason to have already fallen into a depression, for quickly escaping from it. It is not, however, satisfactory to end the discussion merely with such vague, general conclusions as this. People will insist upon asking, what are we to do about it? and this question cannot be ignored.

Some of the more detailed practical conclusions which emerge from our argument have been implicit in earlier discussions, but may briefly be recapitulated here. The importance of educational policy has already been clearly indicated. Further, the limits of credit policy have also been suggested. So far as it can be made effective for the purpose, a credit policy, making possible the price movements which will give to entrepreneurs correct indications as to the directions in which it is desirable to retard or to accelerate the flow of capital, is an essential condition of stability in a progressive capitalist economy; beyond this, credit policy, as ordinarily understood, cannot go. If dislocations are caused by the refusal of entrepreneurs to direct capital in the right direction, quantitative credit policy is quite ineffective to correct their errors. "An increase of general purchasing power would not, in the long run, help the grower of a product or the manufacturer of an article whose specialty was in process of being superseded." [1] Indeed it may be positively dangerous if it creates a situation in which the need for readjustments and transfers appears for the time being to be less urgent. [2]

It should now also be abundantly clear that whatever else is needed to-day, we certainly do not need any more organised large-scale land settlement. The world as a whole already has more farmers than it needs, and farming in general is seriously burdened by over-capitalisation. As time goes on, farming no doubt will continue to receive a substantial share of the community's new savings. It would be a mistake, if, suddenly seized of the folly of pouring excessive supplies of capital into farming, we were to run to the opposite extreme and starve farming industries of the capital supplies which they need, but it would be easier to correct an error which gave us too few farmers than one which gave us too many. There are, however, in any event, so many influences pressing in the direction of

---

[1] *Statist*, June 9, 1934, p. 953.

[2] Cf. P. W. Martin, *Unemployment and Purchasing Power*, pp. 78-9: "A falling off in demand for a *particular* variety of goods coupled with a *general* deficiency of purchasing power means that the men and women thrown out of work will not be likely to find employment elsewhere. With purchasing power for goods in general continuously maintained, a falling off in the demand for a particular variety of goods implies a corresponding increase in demand for some other variety of goods, so that the plight of those unemployed is decidedly less serious. But the fact remains that adequate purchasing power for goods in general will not prevent certain trades from shrinking, and, although this will be compensated by expansion elsewhere, the change over from one type of work to another cannot be effected without great individual hardship and considerable loss."

over-development of primary production that we shall commit no serious error if we affirm without qualification that the attention of investors to-day should be turned definitely in other directions.

Radical changes are also necessary in the outlook which became dominant during the nineteenth century towards migration. Some of the opinions which are current on this subject to-day illustrate better than anything else the common tendency to suppose that it is desirable for social or political reasons to stimulate certain types of production without paying any serious attention to the question whether a world which is growing in wealth actually wants more of those types or not. Both in England and elsewhere, for example, people continue to talk of large-scale migration as an essential part of any policy designed to make the most of the world's resources. They seem to forget that large-scale migration during the nineteenth century was desirable and advantageous to the migrants, because world conditions then made it necessary for the benefit of the industrial populations of the Old World to increase rapidly the output of food and raw materials from the New. The urgency of this need has now much diminished, and the advantages of large-scale migration have been correspondingly reduced. Indeed if many of the "tertiary" products are likely to flourish most in the old-established centres of culture and civilisation, it is desirable that the flow of migration should dry up altogether or even be actually reversed. It is significant that "in recent years emigration from industrial countries has been smaller than from agrarian countries: the limits upon the productive capacity of the former are much more elastic than for the latter".[1] On the whole

[1] Franz Eulenberg, *Encyclopaedia of Social Sciences*, vol. viii. p. 197.

the types of work characteristic of the secondary and tertiary stages of development are likely to be less definitely localised by the nature of the environment in which they must be carried on than the industries of the primary stage. It will therefore tend to become easier in each community to organise the production of the newer goods and services without any large-scale transfer of population to the areas where the essential natural resources are to be found.

But important as these and similar considerations are, it may reasonably be objected that they still fail to get to the root of the matter. Are we not in fact compelled to say something about the organisation of industry as a whole in the light of the principles of adjustment which we have elaborated? It has been pointed out that the character of the adjustments which are necessary in a progressive economy is independent of the machinery used to bring the adjustments about. But it is also necessary to ask what type of machinery is in fact likely to be most effective for this purpose.

In the past the adjustments which we have been describing have been carried through by the ordinary machinery of the capitalist system with which the world as a whole is now fairly familiar. In recent years, as we have seen, there has been increasing reluctance to allow this machinery to function according to plan. The capitalist has often shown little understanding of the foundations of the system which it is his business to work; it sometimes seems that he has lost the confidence in himself which braced him for the business adventures of the past. Instead of making the bold experiments which were characteristic of the capitalist of earlier generations, he tends much more to seek security for himself by the maintenance of the *status quo*. The one thing, it has been said, about which the self-styled "sound business man" knows nothing is sound business. Is it possible to persuade any considerable proportion of business men to appreciate what material progress means, and is it possible to get them to act upon their knowledge? It would no doubt be unfair to saddle the individual saver with full responsibility for the regrettable consequences which follow the general tendency to try to keep things as they are. A man who has only small savings under his control cannot reasonably be expected to take great risks. From the point of view of his own interests, he would be most unwise to do anything of the kind. Unfortunately, however, the combined effects of action which appears definitely in the self-interest of individuals are in this instance equally definitely to the detriment of the community as a whole. Are we to regard this "safety-first" attitude as merely a temporary aberration, or does it indicate a radical decay of the structure of capitalism? Is there any hope of reviving the capitalist faith, or would it be like Julian trying to revive the dead gods of ancient Greece?[1]

[1] An interesting subject for speculation is offered by the thesis of Max Weber (*The Protestant Ethic and the Spirit of Capitalism*) which suggested that "Capitalism was the social counterpart of Calvinist theology". The material progress of the seventeenth century and later would have been impossible without a definite breach with the codes of social and economic morality of the Middle Ages. The breach with traditionalism and confidence against the flood of mistrust and indignation which such a breach was certain to provoke demanded ethical qualities of an unusual order. According to Weber, Calvinism provided a strong religious foundation on which these could be based, at the same time as it gave a religious sanction to exactly the activities which were necessary to enable a capitalist system to initiate and carry through the rapid industrial changes. The religious revolution of the sixteenth century provided a framework of sentiments and ideals which made possible the hardness and tenacity which were essential for the birth

Much of the argument might be indeed interpreted as a polemic in favour of pure economic liberalism, and it has in fact sometimes been applied in that sense.[1] It can easily be fitted into Cassel's criticisms of monopolism[2] and of the general liberal theory which explains the crisis as the consequences of excessive rigidity in the economic structure. Changes in the character of industry, it is argued, call for flexibility of costs and prices. This flexibility is checked by price fixation, cartels, wage regulation, etc., and the whole economic structure is accordingly thrown out of gear. The influences to which we have drawn attention might be regarded merely as partial explanations of this dislocating rigidity.[3]

Pure economic liberalism is, however, by no means an inevitable logical deduction from our argument. Our thesis is not a thinly disguised plea for *laissez-faire*. The arguments of apologists for *laissez-faire* are in fact usually sterile largely for the reason that they persistently neglect the fundamental prejudices which

of a capitalist society. Weber's thesis is perhaps exaggerated and one-sided, but it is permissible to suggest that there may be a connection between the inertia of many modern capitalists and the fact that they often lack any general philosophy of life. The continuous care and readiness to face risks, which are necessary for material progress, are unlikely to be practised without some fundamental conviction, some general philosophy of life, which will make such activities appear worth while.

[1] Cf. Robbins, *The Great Depression.*

[2] Cf. *Recent Monopolistic Tendencies in Industry and Trade,* 1927.

[3] Hansen's position further illustrates this point of view. In discussing technological unemployment (*American Economic Review,* Supplement 1932, pp. 25-36) he argues that "there is no assurance that the displaced labour will, in all cases, be reabsorbed unless we assume a flexible economic structure, a flexible system of prices and wage rates". The price of agents of production must fall to the point at which it would be profitable for entrepreneurs to employ them; technological unemployment therefore can be avoided, only if flexible wage and credit policies are pursued.

our argument has been designed to bring into the light. In the twentieth century the advocate of so-called "liberal" economic theory is in fact usually reduced to the lamentation, "How easily everything would work if only everything were different". A purely *laissez-faire* organisation might work perfectly, if everybody would quickly make the appropriate responses to variations in relative prices and in relative profits. In real life people refuse to do this, and the grounds for their refusal, however irrational they may be, are as deeply rooted in our society as are the fundamental truths of "liberal" economics. If we merely go about deploring their refusal, when there is not the slightest chance of any general or wide-spread change of attitude, we are wasting our time in activities which are no more useful than crying for the moon. People who are attracted by the formal liberty of a *laissez-faire* system often make a great deal of an alleged contrast between the effects of Government interference and of private enterprise. There are few discussions likely to be more superficial than this. Business men often talk as if there were on the one hand a group of ardent entrepreneurs and capitalists, anxious to "obey the law of supply and demand" and to take the risks of innovation, un-hampered by any sort of State control, and on the other hand a group of politicians eager to impose upon the innocent business man all sorts of irritating and deadening restrictions. For the most part, however, the restrictions which are imposed, whether well-advised or not, are the direct expression of the re-luctance of important groups in the community, both business men and others, to face the necessity for the adaptations which have here been discussed. If such reluctance is sin, there are few business men who can afford to cast the first stone at the other sections of the community whom they sometimes so harshly criticise. Government regulation is not something which has its origin outside the region controlled by private enterprise. It finds indeed some of its most powerful roots in the prejudices and fears of change of those very people who eagerly denounce it.[1]

The doctrine of pure liberalism no doubt has powerful attractions. But it is not easy to embrace it unless we are prepared to ignore important and inescapable facts. Its attraction is indeed in large part aesthetic.[2] It appeals to people who take an aesthetic pleasure in the elaboration of a neat, well-balanced, well-rounded system of principles, and interrelations of cause and

[1] Much of Professor Robbins's powerful argument in favour of "the restoration of capitalism" is vitiated by his failure to pay sufficient attention to these fundamental points (cf. *The Great Depression, passim*). "The aim of governmental policy in regard to industry", he says, "must be to create a field in which the forces of enterprise and the disposal of resources are once more allowed to be governed by the market" (p. 193), and he makes a plea that we should not despair of the power of reason to ensure the acceptance of sound policy. As he puts it, "in the short run ideas are unimportant and ineffective, but in the long run they rule the world" (p. 200). Professor Robbins is protesting against the controls and protective devices which in his view check the effective operation of the influences of the market, but it is surely a mistake to suppose that the dominance of the ideas which he is attacking is merely the result of the work of "detached and isolated thinkers". The essential fact is that powerful vested interests find themselves faced with the risk of loss, and ideas of protection have developed directly from the desires of these interests to insure themselves against these risks. These interests and these desires are fundamental facts in the situation; if we ignore their existence or imagine that people will, without the application of some powerful pressure, abandon the practices to which their fears of loss impel them, we are living in a world of make-believe.

[2] Cf. F. C. Benham, *Go Back to Gold*: "As an economist, I have learned to love the way in which a flexible economic system in which prices and wages are quite free to move and the quantity of money is fixed, automatically responds to changed conditions, to changes in consumers' wants, in methods of production, and in factors external to man."

effect. The value of such intellectual exercises is often great, and even if they are found to be inadequate, it is always a mistake to imagine that the conclusions suggested by such an analysis can safely be thrown overboard altogether. Many of the principles of such a theory are true, though at the same time incomplete, and a wider, more realistic theory cannot afford to ignore them. But the "elegance" of any body of doctrine is an inadequate excuse for refusing to push further ahead and endeavouring to include in our analysis all and not merely some of the facts which are relevant to modern economic development. This task is certainly difficult and the results are unlikely to make the same appeal to our aesthetic sensibilities, but a truly scientific outlook can scarcely be content with anything less.

If the capitalist faith is to be revived, pure liberalism will help us little.[1] We must rather examine whether it is possible by the development of appropriate institutions to create an environment within which it will be easier than it is to-day to persuade a sufficiently large number of capitalists of the value and necessity of the adaptations which we have been describing. Reluctance to change is often unintelligent, and the risks associated with it exaggerated. Some of the losses which are feared are genuine losses but others are imaginary, and if a sufficient number of entrepreneurs can be persuaded to take far-sighted views of the future, they might be able to swing the others into line. Even if the problems of adaptation and transfer were

[1] Cf. R. W. Souter, *Prolegomena to Relativity Economics*, p. 164: "If the desire for stability and security is to be even partially satisfied, the necessary and inevitable price must be paid in a progressive modification of our fundamental institutions".

not completely solved in this way, the worst risks of instability might be avoided and the existing economic order enabled to proceed, if not on a perfectly even keel at least without the danger of complete shipwreck.

Hopes are sometimes entertained that the risk of errors in investment would be diminished if the investor paid more time and attention to the care of his savings. Apart from the fact, already mentioned, that by himself he is seldom in a position to follow effectively a sound investment policy, many individual investors feel averse, and for very good reasons, to attempting to convert themselves into scientifically managed investment trusts. They have what appear to them to be more interesting and more important things to do, and who is to say that they are wrong? If a solution is to be found anywhere within the framework of a capitalist economy, it must be sought along lines which will concentrate the responsibility for decisions in the hands of specialists and not dissipate responsibility over the whole vast heterogeneous group of people who have a little money to invest.

The essential problem here, it has already been pointed out, is that of harmonising the natural reluctance of the small investor to take risks, which from the standpoint of his own interests appear excessive, with the necessity of making available an increased share of the community's savings for enterprises with a degree of risk attached which is higher than the average of the past. Is it possible to devise any machinery which will surmount this difficulty, which will guarantee the small investor the security which he naturally and properly desires, and at the same time will make available adequate supplies of capital in new and relatively untried fields of production?

In this connection several proposals have been put forward which deserve consideration. It is not possible here to expound or criticise them elaborately, but a brief discussion will be useful for bringing into clearer relief the nature of the fundamental problem.

Our earlier discussion of the Macmillan Committee's comment upon the inadequacy of the English capital market has already suggested one method for maintaining stability in a progressive capitalist economy. The problem is essentially that of bringing into more direct contact that part of the savings of the community which is now inadequately utilised with the knowledge of the new and improved methods of production which are constantly being developed, and the managerial skill which is available for administering the units of production which are to use these methods. The crux of the situation to-day is that the individuals who take the first steps in experimenting with new investments are very likely to lose their money, while those who come after, when recovery is well under way, may do very well. In these circumstances naturally no one is willing to take the first step, but, equally naturally, so long as no one is willing to take the first step, it is impossible for anyone to come after, and the process of recovery therefore lags behind.

The Macmillan Committee suggested the establishment of a financial organisation with special responsibility for the provision of intermediate credit for those types of business enterprise for which in the past inadequate facilities had been available in the English capital market,[1] and certain important experiments

---

[1] Cf. Sir W. C. Dampier, *Lloyds Bank Monthly Review*, September 1933, p. 368: "There does seem a need for easier facilities for the financing of approved inventions and other new industries at an early stage,

have been made in England recently along these lines. Of these experiments the most interesting are Credit for Industries, Ltd., and the Charterhouse Industrial Development Company. Credit for Industries has been launched by the United Dominions Trust, of which the Bank of England is the principal shareholder, and is also supported by the large commercial banks. The original capital is to be £250,000, and further finance will be available by the company's own borrowings from the banks or otherwise, and the issue of debentures or short-dated securities. The Charterhouse Industrial Development Company has been formed by the Charterhouse Investment Trust, with a capital of £500,000, and has a similar objective in the provision of capital for those types of business unit of small and medium size which in the past have been inadequately supplied. Credit for Industries proposes to advance loan capital only, but the Charterhouse Industrial Development Company will also take up shares. Neither of these companies intends, however, to concern itself with experiments in new types of activity, confining attention rather to the expansion of existing businesses. The significance of proposals of this kind is that they concentrate attention on that part of the machinery of production where we may most hopefully look for effective action in adjusting the organisation as a whole to the requirements of progress. If the progress of

before they are ripe for a public appeal. Perhaps a corporation under the common control of the Joint Stock Banks might undertake this work. A Committee of men of science might advise, or recommend someone who could advise on the mere technical soundness of new ideas. They would not be fitted or expected to deal with the economic prospects, which could only be estimated by business men conversant with the particular industry involved. By some such interlocking scheme, new industries—necessary in times when old ones are depressed and savings superabundant—might be helped into being."

science renders a number of wheat-farmers superfluous
in their present occupation, the position appears rather
desperate when we approach it directly from the displaced wheat-farmer's end. If, however, we start at the
other end and by an improved organisation of the community's stream of savings facilitate the development
of new industrial developments, we may by a series of
transfers, so to speak, siphon the "superfluous" farmer
out of his present field of activity, so that he finds he is
definitely wanted somewhere else and accordingly feels
the pains of transfer less acutely.

A large organisation of this kind could face with
equanimity the prospect of some early failures. The
fear of loss acts as a natural deterrent to the small investor, but a larger organisation could afford to take
the longer views which the situation demands. The
effective operation of such machinery as is here suggested almost inevitably demands a closer co-operation
between banks, both central and trading, and industrial units than would conform to the traditions of
English banking. But if material progress demands
fundamental changes in the structure of industry, it is
essential that banking should adapt itself to these
changes. Especially is it necessary to build up an efficient organisation for maintaining a continuous survey
of industry as a whole so that the directions in which
further capital investment was desirable could be
readily identified. Trading banks already have at their
disposal much information which is relevant to this
purpose, but no bank has information which covers the
whole field. To many bankers the type of business in
which they specialise seems not to demand that complete and thoroughgoing survey of industry as a whole
which is necessary when we are considering not the

allocation of short-term credit to industrial units which are already in full working order, but the provision of long-term capital for the extension of permanent equipment or for new industrial units. As the Macmillan Report put it, "no financial institution which assumed the responsibility of vouching for industrial issues could do so on the basis of an isolated connection formed with the industry solely for this purpose. Responsibility of this kind can only be the outcome of a close and continuous relationship with the industry concerned, different in kind from the relationship now existing between the Joint Stock banks and industry" (p. 168). Even for ordinary banking business of the traditional kind, such an adequate information service would have great value.

A close relationship with the central bank would be especially valuable for meeting the powerful prejudice in favour of business secrecy. A business unit may object to having its affairs disclosed to rivals, but there can be no reasonable objection to a central co-ordinating organisation maintaining a continuous contact with the development of industries as a whole. It is as much to the interest of people already engaged in an industry that superfluous rivals should be warned off as it is to the interest of new investors that they should be advised against risking the loss of their capital in industries which are sufficiently developed, and the central bank, in consequence of its status as a co-ordinator of the banking system, is in an unusually favourable position for initiating the collection of such information, without arousing the suspicions of individual units that their secrets were to be made public.

The same set of ideas has been worked out in a different framework in the ingenious scheme of M. Roger

Alheine, a French banker, for regulating by methods of insurance the ebb and flow of capital in industry, so that it should be withdrawn from industries which are over-producing and transferred to industries which are not meeting demand adequately.[1] At present the price of "lending" and the price of "risk" are determined in the same market and in one transaction, and by estimates which are often quite arbitrary, depending upon the judgment of the promoters, the mood of the market and the ease with which the securities can be resold. M. Alheine wishes to separate the two operations. He wants the banks or money market to have the placing of the securities at a rate determined only by the abundance or scarcity of capital at the time, and the "risk" to be dealt with by credit insurance companies, who would cover the risk of capital loss by payment of a suitable premium. A firm desiring fresh capital would go to the insurance company and ask for insurance against the repayment of this capital at maturity date. If, after examining the firm's financial position and prospects, its markets, and its competitive powers, the insurance company accepts the insurance, the firm would then be able, armed with this guarantee of capital repayment, to place its shares at a rate of interest or at an issuing price which ignores the element of risk altogether. Theoretically the difference will compensate the borrower for the premium paid to the insurance company.

Any particular insurance company engaged in such business might shortly find itself overloaded with the risks of all the enterprises of a particular industry or a

---

[1] *La Paix Financière*, Paris, 1932. Cf. Francis Delaisi, "Causes and Cure for State Control", *World Trade*, October 1932–February 1933. See also *Manchester Guardian Commercial*, February 25, 1933, p. 148.

particular region, and must therefore have recourse to reinsurance with a Reinsurance Company of national scope. This reinsurance company would be more concerned with a broad national outlook on market tendencies than with the details of each risk reinsured with it. It would require to know those industries which were producing in excess of demand and those which could usefully apply new capital for development. Its reinsurance rates would reflect back on the premiums quoted by the primary insurance company.

The national Reinsurance Companies would, in turn, hedge their risks by further reinsurance with International Insurance Companies, chiefly concerned with world price movements of raw materials, foreign currencies and foreign-market risks, and M. Alheine proposes further to strengthen the capital of the International Insurance Companies by a guarantee of the participating States which he argues would be far less onerous for Governments than the state of affairs actually in operation to-day, when they are obliged to spend hundreds of millions, without having made any provision for such expenditure, on supporting banks which have got into difficulties and industries which are bankrupt.

It is doubtful whether this proposal does not ignore the fundamental distinctions which exist between different types of risk. The risks of capital loss are not of the kind for which actuarial calculations are possible. Such value as M. Alheine's proposal may have lies not in the idea of insuring against capital losses but in the implied suggestion that investment requires a more careful and far-reaching survey of the whole economy than is usually possible to-day. Especially in a complex and highly organised society we need "a kind of economic traffic-signal, the red and green lights regulating the movement of capital and preventing production from getting blocked".

A third avenue of approach towards the maintenance of equilibrium in a progressive capitalist economy is opened up when we consider the possibility of stabilising demand in that part of the structure where the very fact of growing wealth most obviously threatens us with chronic instability, the part which is concerned with the production of the numerous miscellaneous goods and services, the "tertiary" products which members of a wealthy community can afford to purchase. The modern development of high-power advertising is a device designed to introduce some stability into this ever-fluctuating stream of demand, but for this purpose it is highly unsatisfactory, as often as not indeed increasing rather than diminishing the amplitude of the fluctuations. Advertising is an expression of a purely individual interest in stability, and where several individuals are struggling violently for stability for themselves the final result may be greatly increased instability for everybody. From the point of view of general stability, it may matter little whether a particular market is dominated by A, B or C or whether it is shared by the three according to some arbitrarily determined ratios. But from the point of view of A, B and C themselves, these matters are of the greatest importance and their active advertising campaigns may be so successful in stimulating swings of demand from one producer to another that general stability entirely disappears.

In these circumstances it is worth while considering whether an extension of communal control in the field of "tertiary" production might not facilitate the maintenance of stability in other fields which were left to ordinary individualist activity. The type of service which is needed in the "tertiary" stage is often one for which the ordinary machinery of capital provision requires somewhat violent adaptation before it can be applied effectively. Everyone is familiar with the conditions which make farming an unsuitable field for joint-stock enterprise. Different circumstances make many of the "tertiary" types of production equally unsuitable for financing of this kind. The alternative methods of finance which it is desirable to develop are unlikely to be the same, but a strong case can be made for State provision of capital for some of the "tertiary" services, together with the financing of any deficits out of taxation. This would in effect be an attempt to stabilise demand by compelling people to purchase certain services whether they wished to or not. This already has been done quite extensively in the provision of education, of parks and libraries, and in some countries has been further extended to include music, the theatre and other services. A still further extension of this trend both in scale and in the range of its objects may be an essential condition for the maintenance of stability in the capitalist system as a whole.

The growing importance of organisations like the Rockefeller and Carnegie Foundations in America, the Carlsberg Foundation in Denmark, and similar institutions elsewhere suggests another line of development which points in the same direction. While economic progress itself depends upon the growth of knowledge, it also makes it easier, and certainly more desirable, to devote a larger proportion of the world's resources to encouraging the same trend. Scientific research is not, however, a service which can easily be organised on the basis of a commercial demand. The Rockefeller and similar Foundations offer an alternative method of organisation. In effect part of the community's savings is abstracted from the normal channels of investment into which they would otherwise tend to flow, and are made available instead for persons presumed to be skilled in the search for knowledge.

Proposals for further extensions of State provision of "tertiary" products do not necessarily mean that we think it proper to compel people to buy what other people think will be good for them, but rest rather on the belief that unless some control of this kind is exercised the economic structure will be so much upset that the freedom of consumers in other parts of the field will disappear altogether because they will lack the income which is necessary to make their freedom of choice effective. To-day consumers are free to spend £100,000 on A, and capital and labour are accordingly organised to produce an adequate supply of A. Next year there may be a violent swing of demand to B. The capital and labour which have in the meantime become specialised in the production of A are left high and dry, while efforts are being made to stimulate industry B, from which in the following year demand may recede just as rapidly. The whole structure might be more stable, and consumers generally have more real freedom, if the £100,000 had been abstracted from their incomes by the State and applied instead to the purchase of some other services organised and supplied on a communal basis.

CHAPTER XI

A CHALLENGE TO CAPITALISM

IF individual entrepreneurs in general refuse to face their responsibilities, can we reasonably anticipate better results from planning? The word "planning" has in recent years had such an attractive ring that it has been widely used as a means of winning support for all sorts of activities and policies which at bottom have very little or nothing in common, and it is doubtful whether the word any longer serves a useful purpose as an instrument for aiding intelligent discussion. From the standpoint of the argument which has been developed in this book, the important point is that the degree of success which it is reasonable to expect from any plan depends directly on the extent to which the planners appreciate the urgency of the need for constant change and adaptation in the structure of production as a whole. It is largely because so many planners are much more concerned about stabilising the *status quo*, at least in the industries with which they are most closely associated, that it is quite consistent to combine a hearty approval of planning in general with a profound scepticism about nearly all concrete specific plans. Even when planners do visualise change, it is usually change in the wrong direction. Instead of aiming at an expansion of production of the things which people with rising incomes are likely to want, planners in real life are often much more anxious to encourage more food production, which is certain to cause further serious dislocation. There is no virtue in planning as such; the results of a plan based on faulty foundations might be worse than the results of not planning at all.

Even if all the ideas which have been briefly described were adopted, it is still possible that the adjustments which would thereby be facilitated will not be enough, or that the resistance of vested interests to change may be so powerful as to prevent the intelligent application of the ideas. The strength of the tradition in favour of high incomes for business executives may be illustrated from one objection raised against a proposal for another experiment on similar lines to Credit for Industries. It would be impossible to get the right man to manage such a concern, it was said, under £7500 per annum, which was obviously a figure which no such company could afford to offer. If all industrial experiments were to be ruled out which could not pay a manager £7500 per annum, it is possible that material progress would be finally and irrevocably checked.[1]

If for any reason it is impossible to reconcile the clash of opposing interests, have we any alternative open to us other than to throw overboard completely existing economic institutions and in their place to set up some centralised control which will compel the rational distribution of capital? It is the central thesis of the communist case that action of this kind

[1] Cf. *Economist*, October 27, 1934: "It is only if the propertied classes in the democratic countries are prepared to accept peacefully some mitigation of economic inequality that those countries can honestly congratulate themselves on the enjoyment of freedom, and cast stones at a Soviet tyranny which crushes it in the name of equality".

will eventually be forced upon us. Capitalists will refuse to do the sensible actions which an analysis of the economy as a whole shows to be necessary because these actions will appear contrary to their own personal and group interests. Sensible action will be impossible unless control is taken out of the hands of people who find that sensible action conflicts with their own interests.

To suggest that socialist or communist control may be necessary to facilitate enjoyment of the fruits of material progress is certainly entirely contrary to much popular thought on this subject. It is often argued that capitalism is the instrument of progress encouraging men to take risks by offering them the undivided control of the gains which their investments bring them, while socialism is attacked as a system likely to discourage progress and create a dull monotony from which all change was excluded. The twentieth-century capitalist, however, refuses to behave in accordance with this theory; he refuses to allow himself to become an instrument of progress. Instead of taking risks, he bends his energies rather to conserving positions which have already been gained. According to a recent English writer, "a hundred years ago, when great overseas markets were being opened up and huge transformations of economic life were ripe for accomplishment as soon as feudal restrictions (Corn Laws and the like) could be shaken off, the business man was not the man of caution but the man of adventure. The feudal opposition to business men's plans purposed to do nothing at all but to maintain the existing order of things in the countryside. To-day, however, the business man for the most part is the opponent of changes. Where great and rapid transformations have been accomplished in the last five years, whether in our own country (the grid, the marketing boards, the sugar industry) or in other countries (land reclamation in Italy, the Muscle Shoals Scheme in the United States, the Shannon Scheme in Ireland, the Turk-Sib Railway in Russia), not business men but Governments have been the active promoters. The business man's area has been that of existing economic conditions, which he has wished to see maintained in an orderly permanence. Business men who were not conservative in this wide sense have often turned out to be adventurers in the narrow sense." [1] Not all the adventurous schemes referred to were well conceived, or in harmony with the requirements of material progress, but the important truth remains that the business man has shown himself more and more reluctant to carry out his peculiar functions of taking risks and trying out new markets and new methods of production. In these circumstances it is inevitable that the case in favour of some alternative economic system should appear to be much strengthened. "The inability of the competitive system to effect an accurate balancing of the costs and the benefits of change is", according to a recent American writer, "perhaps the strongest argument in favour of communism or some form of socialism." [2] An inaccurate balancing of the costs and the benefits of change may sometimes show itself in the infliction of serious damage upon workers overwhelmed by the ruthless demands for rapid adaptation which are often presented to them. But where the costs are more directly borne by the entrepreneur himself, he may tip the balance the other way, and instead of pushing forward with new ideas too

---

[1] *Manchester Guardian Commercial*, March 8, 1934.
[2] Slichter, *American Economic Review*, Supplement, 1932, p. 41.

rapidly, he may by his excessive conservatism completely bar the road to material progress.

We have already suggested one skeleton outline of world economic history in three stages, one of which is still for the most part in the future. The argument here may be illustrated by another skeleton outline showing a different set of three stages. In the primitive poorest stage, the stage in which the members of many savage tribes are still living, the supply of the most essential products is so meagre that some rationing of supplies, some measure of communism is inevitable. More advanced communities return to this stage in part or in whole, when some sudden catastrophe drastically diminishes supplies and imposes poverty on all. Shipwrecked crews, the inhabitants of beleaguered cities, to some extent all the inhabitants of advanced modern countries when they are engaged in war, practise a measure of communism, because by no other method is it possible to ensure that poverty will not be overwhelmingly concentrated on certain members of the group. When some progress has been made in the arts of agriculture and of production generally, we enter the second stage where primitive communism ceases to be appropriate. It now becomes necessary to encourage individual initiative and experimentation. Communism might have too cramping an effect, when it was a question of trying out new methods of work. Risks must be taken and individuals are encouraged to do this by the lure of profit. When still further progress has been made and higher levels of average income have been reached, the lure of profit gradually loses its effectiveness. On account of growing sensitivity to the value of personal security, on account of the instability of demand and for other reasons, the risks associated with new ventures appear to those who in a capitalist economy should undertake them so overwhelming that they refuse to face them. In these conditions some form of communism may become necessary, not to grapple with the problems of poverty but rather to facilitate the rational organisation of plenty.

When we are threatened with disaster because an important group in our society persistently refuses to take the risks which are its peculiar function, we can, if rational persuasion fails to give an adequate inducement, transfer their function to someone else. If investors hesitate about the whole-hearted adoption of a wise investment policy, because it may mean the loss of part of the capital which they already control, the effects of such hesitation will be diminished if there are no individual investors who can be liable to such fears of loss. The root of the labourer's objection to change lies not so much in his devotion to his customary work as in his devotion to his customary income. If he can be safeguarded against the risks associated to-day with the transition from one kind of work to another, there will usually be very little objection to change as such.

It is impossible to discuss exhaustively all the issues which are involved here. We are asking questions now, not answering them. While a socialist or communist economy would be freed from some of the most important influences which to-day check desirable adaptations in the structure of production, we cannot light-heartedly assume without further question that a socialist or communist economy would in fact make all the necessary adaptations promptly or effectively. It is, however, of the greatest importance for capitalists to understand from what direction the most fundamental and telling criticisms of the capitalist system are now likely to come. In dealing with each specific current problem, it is necessary to re-orientate our thought so that it shall be considered in the light of the needs of a community which is capable of rapid material progress. As with other criticisms of capitalism, the only effective answer is actually to perform the tasks which the communist alleges are impossible, actually to carry through the adaptations the absence of which to-day is both checking the trend towards material progress and threatening to upset completely our traditional economic institutions. The responsibility for refuting the argument that privilege will prevent wise action must rest with the people who occupy privileged positions. The capitalist can no longer expect to be taken seriously if he merely *argues* that capitalism encourages initiative and experimentation. He must go further than argument; he must act. It is his responsibility to show by his day-to-day actions that capitalism in the twentieth century is not inconsistent with a full and wide enjoyment of the fruits of material progress. It is no longer even a good debating point against proposals for the reform of economic organisation to say that "while they might be good in theory, they are likely to be bad in practice"; it would be equally fair to say of most of the defences which are put up to-day for twentieth-century capitalism that "they are only good in theory". Actual practice reveals little conformity with theory, and the capitalist cannot be allowed indefinitely to refuse to shoulder the responsibility for bringing the two into line.

INDEX

231

THE END